PENGUIN BOOK
BBC BOOKS

GREEK AS A TREAT

Peter France was a late convert to classical Greece. It was not until 1987 that he first visited the Greek islands, when he immediately lost all reason and bought a tiny house on Patmos, where he spends six months of every year wrestling with the language and enjoying the ouzo and literature.

The first fifteen years of his working life were spent as a colonial civil servant on the Fiji Islands, where he rose to Permanent Secretary. After a spell as an academic working on his thesis, which was published under the title *The Charter of the Land*, he started a new career in the media, first in radio, where he launched (and presented) *Kaleidoscope*, and then in television. His television credits include *Everyman*, for which he was writer and presenter for ten years, *Heart of the Matter*, *Global Report*, *The Natural World*, *Wildlife on One*, *Horizon* and *Time-watch*. He wrote and presented the five-part documentary series *The Birth of Europe* for Radio 4 in 1991, and has published *The Rape of Egypt*.

Greek as a Treat accompanies six programmes first broadcast on Radio 4 in spring 1993.

PETER FRANCE

———————

GREEK AS A TREAT

AN INTRODUCTION TO
THE CLASSICS

PENGUIN BOOKS
BBC BOOKS

PENGUIN BOOKS
BBC BOOKS

Published by the Penguin Group and BBC Enterprises Ltd
Penguin Books Ltd, 27 Wrights Lane, London W8 5TZ, England
Penguin Books USA Inc., 375 Hudson Street, New York, New York 10014, USA
Penguin Books Australia Ltd, Ringwood, Victoria, Australia
Penguin Books Canada Ltd, 10 Alcorn Avenue, Toronto, Ontario, Canada M4V 3B2
Penguin Books (NZ) Ltd, 182–190 Wairau Road, Auckland 10, New Zealand

Penguin Books Ltd, Registered Offices: Harmondsworth, Middlesex, England

First published by BBC Books, a division of BBC Enterprises Ltd 1993
Published in Penguin Books 1994
3 5 7 9 10 8 6 4 2

Printed in England by Clays Ltd, St Ives plc

ACKNOWLEDGEMENTS

This book was written on the island of Patmos and I am very grateful to the Headmaster of the Patmian School for the use of books in Modern Greek and to the librarian of the Holy Monastery of St John Theologian for permission to work there. Carraigh B. Thomson of Agrio Livadi generously made available his library and critical faculties from which I greatly benefitted and I made the most of the advice of my friend the painter Vasilis Kipreos who loves Greek culture.

Swan Hellenic Cruises very kindly shipped me around the sites and I learned a lot from their guest lecturers Colin Badcock and the Revd. Robert Glen. In Athens, I was encouraged by Eleni Kipreos of the New Forms Gallery and Mary Michaelidou of the Ministry of Culture.

Professor Sir Kenneth Dover, at St Andrews, was generous with his time and advice and Professor Bernard Williams, in Oxford, set me right not only about Greek ethics but about Greek drama. Professor Dan O'Connor of Exeter and Dr Oliver Taplin of Magdalen College, Oxford, kindly shaped my early ideas and Dr Stephen Instone of London University the later ones. Above all, I am grateful to Dr Peter Jones of Newcastle University whose enthusiasm for his subject would ignite a passion for Aeschylus in the breast of an aardvark. He kindly cast an eye over the manuscript and pointed out its more obvious howlers. For the ones that remain I am, of course, completely responsible.

I am very grateful to Penguin Books for permission to quote extracts from the following: Aeschylus, *The Oresteian Trilogy*, trans. by Philip Vellacott; Aristophanes, *Birds and other plays*, trans. by David Barrett; Aristophanes, *Lysistrata and other plays*, trans. by Alan H. Sommerstein; Euripides, *Medea and other plays*, trans. by Philip Vellacott; Herodotus, *The Histories*, trans. by Aubrey de Selincourt, revised by A. R. Burn; Homer, *The Iliad*, trans. by Martin Hammond; Homer, *The Odyssey*, trans. by E. V. Rieu, revised by D. C. H. Rieu in consultation with Peter V. Jones; Plato, *The Last Days of Socrates*, trans. by Hugh Tredennick; Plato, *The Laws*, trans. by Trevor J. Saunders; Sophocles, *Electra and other plays*, trans. E. F. Watling; Thucydides, *History of the Peloponnesian War*, trans. Rex Warner.

CONTENTS

Introduction

Greek, there is no doubt, has lost its grip. There was a time when everybody knew all about it. Everybody, that is, who was anybody. You couldn't become Prime Minister or Director-General of the BBC unless you did. You couldn't even be a doctor, a lawyer or a country parson unless you'd worked your way through a classical education of cold baths and irregular verbs. For centuries British politicians were more likely to be familiar with the social conditions of Athens in the fifth century BC than those of Hackney or Huddersfield in their own time.

But now it's all gone. Our leaders didn't get where they are today by memorizing what somebody said in Greece two and a half thousand years ago. If they think of the classics at all they're likely to be doing a crossword or watching an old film on television. The Marathon, for us, is a Sunday stampede of twenty-five thousand across Westminster Bridge; the Hippocratic Oath is what doctors are occasionally hauled in front of television cameras for breaking – although the papers never tell us what it is; and Platonic means friendship without fun. Our age is in the grip of a general indifference towards classical Greece.

And here, I think, I can enter a special claim as a qualification for writing this book: I never personally shared this general indifference to the Golden Age of Pericles, the Founding Fathers of Democracy, the Birthplace of Classical Art, the Cradle of our European civilization. I simply hated the whole bang shoot. I was, from my schooldays, as near as dammit, Greeceproof.

There were good reasons: Greek was never a load of laughs. Even in the morose curriculum of the school certificate course it touched bottom in terms of entertainment value. In no other subject did so much effort produce so little reward. Greek won and kept its place in our educational system because it was seen as an assault course that would separate the men from the boys. If you could survive it you were made of the right stuff: you could command respect; you were equipped to be a leader of men; you could go ahead and become Governor of the Bank of England or of New South Wales. The study of Greek, announced the Revd Thomas Gaisford from the pulpit of Christ Church in his Christmas sermon for 1855, 'not only elevates above the vulgar herd but also leads not infrequently to positions of considerable emolument'.

There were two reasons why Greek acquired this reputation: it was difficult and it was irrelevant. Only the very brightest students could cope with the intricacies of Greek grammar; most fell at the Bechers Brook of the enclitics or were unseated at the Canal Turn of the second aorist passive. Only the really clever dicks could cope; and those who mastered Greek knew themselves destined for higher things and approached life with an assumption of effortless superiority that the rest of us found hard to take.

In schools where Greek was compulsory it was never thought of with affection – just the opposite. The classics teachers showed their own feelings for the subject by using it as an instrument of punishment: turn up late for prep and you had to get by heart six irregular verbs by the next day. Greek was an alternative to the rod.

The total irrelevance of classical Greek as a dead language was also an invaluable test of character. If a boy could buckle down to cudgelling his brains for four hours a day over something that was going to be of no practical use to him whatever, his sense of duty was clearly masterful enough for him to flourish in the Civil Service, the Church or the Army – where the ability to hurl yourself with energy and enthusiasm into utterly pointless activities has always been an essential qualification for high office. 'Nobody', wrote Shaw, 'can say a word against Greek: it stamps a man at once as an educated gentleman.'

I missed out on all of this in Rastrick Grammar School, Brighouse.

I did Latin. And so it was the Romance languages – French and Italian – that awoke in me the little corner of the Mediterranean that lies hidden in all of us. You know, the bit that responds to warm blue seas and sun-kissed olive groves and golden tenors; to excitement and passion and steaming great plates of pasta – everything blazing with colour and carried to violent and marvellous excess. It all went down very well under the smoky skies of the industrial heart of the West Riding of Yorkshire.

To me the Greeks seemed opposed to life in the fast lane. I had a vague idea that they must put so much effort into mastering their language that they had no energy for anything else. That would explain their middle-aged, middle-class philosophy of doing 'nothing to excess' which was one of their mottos. They even engraved it over the temple of their most famous oracle at Delphi. They took a great pride in moderation, proportion, rationality – the measured life, lived at about two degrees below normal temperature. The Greeks were to blame for that depraved, life-denying, sententious, thoroughly nasty little edict: 'always get up from the table feeling slightly hungry.'

It was this cool rationality of the Greeks that made it possible for them to work what seemed to me to be a minor miracle of sculpture: they could actually carve out naked female figures that we, as school-boys, found totally unarousing. We, who were driven to a frenzy by soft-focus photographs of naked tennis-playing girls whose pubic hair had been tactfully smudged out by the magazine *Health and Efficiency*, could gaze on the fountain nymphs in the municipal park, whose groins were also bald, quite unmoved. I was to learn much later of poor John Ruskin, besotted by the charms of the Greek statues, who was unable to consummate his marriage when he discovered that his bride, unlike the smooth white marble bodies he adored, had pubic hair.

If the aim of classical art was to raise the human spirit to its highest levels, purging the mind of its grosser elements through a careful combination of balance, proportion, and the golden mean, all under the unrelenting control of the reason, I decided I didn't want a bar of it. If the classical Greeks were ruled by seemliness, proportion, balance and moderation, you could keep them.

There were, later on, other alienating influences. As presenter of the BBC arts programme *Kaleidoscope*, I was always finding myself in the canteen dining the critics. Now, one of the rules of broadcasting is never to discuss what you want said on the programme too fully before you go on air because the contributor then feels he's said it already and won't say it again when it matters. So the conversation would often drift around to where we spent our holidays and the guest critics, usually of a sensitive and aesthetic bent, would always go on to recommend a particular Greek island they knew – Athos or Porthos or Aramis – which was quite marvellous, utterly unspoilt and where one could lie for hours in the sun reading Proust with one's friends. I made up my mind never to set foot in Greece for the risk of meeting one of them. I remained as near as humanly possible Greeceproof.

But there was always a nagging problem: if Greek was so hopelessly rational, so negative, so life-denying, how had it managed to excite the imaginations of so many people I admired? Dr Johnson, who could leap out of bed in the middle of the night because he heard there was a party on, once said, 'Greek, sir, is like lace: every man gets as much of it as he can.' Greek studies have been able for centuries, in Gilbert Murray's phrase, 'to intoxicate the keenest minds of Europe'. Both Byron and Shelley, neither of them given to an arid, intellectual, or even rationally balanced view of life, were dotty about the Greeks. The Irish poet Yeats, a man not insensitive to magic and mystery who was never one to let the human reason get out of control in his life, wrote, 'My son is now between nine and ten and should begin Greek at once.' Winston Churchill once sounded forth on how the youth of England should be educated: 'I would make them all learn English; and then I would let the clever ones learn Latin as an honour and Greek as a treat.' Isadora Duncan danced on the Parthenon at dawn in diaphanous veils in honour of the ancient Athenians and Dame Sybil Thorndike was so convinced of the universal appeal of Greek tragedy that she toured the Welsh mining valleys and played Euripides to the astonished miners of Tonypandy.

These enthusiasts, with the exception of Gilbert Murray, were not classical scholars. So their enthusiasm cannot be explained away by suggesting they thought anything so hard to achieve as an understanding of Greek had to be worthwhile and should be inflicted on everybody else; they had no sunk-cost syndrome to explain their obsession with classical Greece.

As Greek had been, for so long and in so many countries, at the heart of the system of education, it seems inadequate to say that it was perpetuated simply because the teachers had been put through it and enjoyed inflicting it on others on the ground that suffering develops character. Either the teaching of Greek from the days of Shakespeare to Winston Churchill has been the most massively successful confidence trick in history or there was something of value in it. And that something of value is in danger of being lost to us today. Classical Greece has receded from us more in the past fifty years than in the preceding five hundred and, like the outer galaxies of the universe, the further away it gets, the greater the speed of the recession.

Perhaps there is a clue to explain this change in the notion of *relevance*, which is never far from the minds of media people today. If you want to sell the idea of a programme in radio or television, or an article in a magazine or newspaper, you won't get far if you say you want to do it because it's worth while. You need a peg to hang it on: an anniversary, a celebrity interest, a new threat to our health or environment, a new cure for an ailment or anxiety that happens to be in the news. These angles will secure a platform, open the columns of our newspapers or the doors of our radio and television studios.

But the condition of Athens in the fifth century BC has no obvious relevance to our present discontents – although, as will often appear in this book, there are surprising parallels between them. And we have to admit the Greek will no longer secure for us those positions of considerable emolument available to classical scholars a hundred years ago. We can't any more rely on it as a passport to an unsackable post with an index-linked pension in the public service; it won't put money in our bank accounts, reduce the mortgage or help towards the laptop computer.

But Greek can reach parts of you that nothing else can touch. I made the discovery late in life and it seems worth while shouting about it a bit so that other people can come across it earlier and get more out of it. Because even if the Greeks won't make us more affluent or help us get more quickly from one place to another, they will, with the smallest of efforts on our part, teach us to find pleasure where we are. Not only can they enrich the periods we spend in stillness and reflection, they can make us enjoy our friends and our food more than we did. Because there were sound reasons why they dominated European culture in later antiquity and why their rediscovery was hailed as a renaissance, a rebirth in human affairs. Those reasons will appear in this book. And they are not only sound, they are as exhilarating today as they ever were. Because this astonishing people, small in numbers, politically disorganized, poverty-stricken, technologically underdeveloped, suddenly discovered, in their remote corner of the Mediterranean, in a burst of light, how to live; what the human mind is for, what is the Good to be sought, the Beauty to be cherished. In fact, they were the first people in the history of the world to raise the question of, and to come close to finding the answer to, what is and what is not, in our human condition, relevant.

This book revives and celebrates some of the lost excitements of what was once called the Golden Age. It is not the work of a classical scholar but a late convert. As such, it is not a careful, balanced, reasoned work. So far as I have been able to check the facts, they are correct as set out, but what I hope to communicate is enthusiasm as well as information. I've used quotations frequently because you can then directly sample what's on offer. If one is not to your taste, skip on to the next. If you like it, then you'll find that just about all the Greeks in this book are available in translation in paperback.

This is a shop window to classical Greece. I've put into it the most exciting and eye-catching products on offer and added a store guide for those who want to step inside.

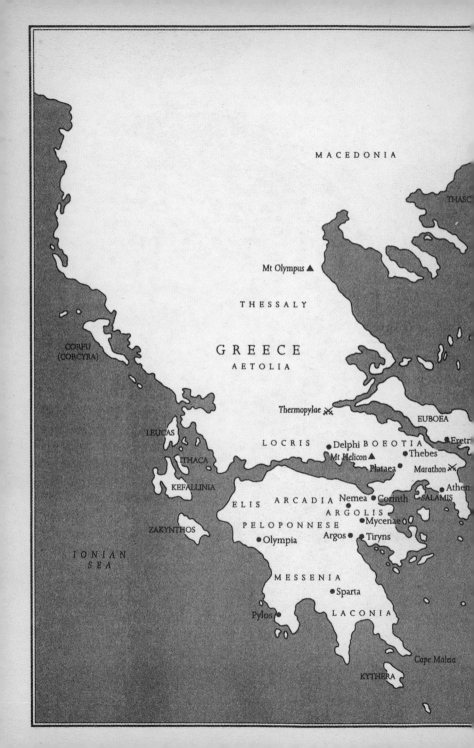

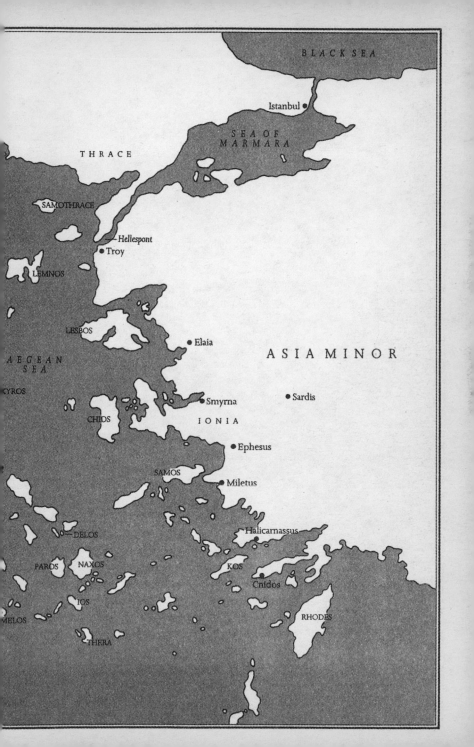

CHAPTER ONE

Academics in Arcadia

It was in the winter of 1991, when the British nation was going through one of its periodic bouts of belt-tightening and the government had decided that no institution, however exalted, should be exempt from the tyranny of good housekeeping, that the University of Oxford announced the closure, on the ground of expense, of Parson's Pleasure.

The national papers carried the news – just: a small paragraph tucked away in the middle pages. If they'd shut down the Bodleian Library there would have been far more fuss. And yet Oxford will never be quite the same without that stretch of riverside meadow on which portly dons used to wander naked in the watery sunlight and exercise their enormous brains by discussing whether the trees around ceased to exist when nobody thought about them and what was the meaning of meaning. We used to punt past the place and wonder at the sight. Ladies were forbidden, so of course we used to take them, in nominal disguises which the more extrovert would tear off with shrieks of delight to abash the pendulous scholars.

There was a story that, on one such occasion, a senior local prelate hastily covered his private parts with an agonized copy of *The Times*, at which his companion, a distinguished classicist, remarked 'I can't speak for *you*, Bishop, but I am known in Oxford by my *face*.'

These distinguished and witty classicists were the inspiration for Parson's Pleasure because the whole idea of wandering about in the buff discussing philosophy was felt to be essentially Greek. It combined the two aspects of Greek life which scholars have celebrated throughout Europe since the Renaissance: the academic and the Arcadian. The celebration tells us more about the scholars than the Greeks.

The Greeks, we are told, discovered Mind. They delighted in seeing the truth through the exercise of their reasoning powers. They were the world's first intellectuals, the original academics. But they were also admired as the natives of the original Arcadia: the first naturists, given to sitting around on rocks in the clear sunlight playing pan-pipes and eating grapes. They were mankind before the fall: natural, spontaneous, joyous, with a great passion for wine and liberty and no inhibitions about sex. Somewhere between cerebral academician and untutored primitive there lurks the true historical Greek; not easy to discover because of the overlaid images of romanticizing historians, but worth seeking out.

The original Academy, which gave its name to so many of our educational institutions, had features in common with Parson's Pleasure. Both were rural places outside the city. The Greek Academy was a large sacred grove with a wall around it in the countryside to the west of Athens. There were twelve sacred olive trees inside, dedicated to Athena, and from them was pressed the oil given as a prize to victors in the Panathenaic Games. There were shrines to many gods and heroes, well-watered gardens and shady avenues where the Athenians used to stroll. Plato founded a school here where the students found the ambience at which our dons of Parsons's Pleasure were aiming. But even in Plato's day, the place was romanticized:

You'll run off to Academe's Park and relax under the sacred olive trees, a wreath of pure white flowers on your head, with a decent, well-mannered companion or two; and you'll share the fragrance of leafy poplar and carefree convolvulus and the joys of spring when the plane tree whispers her love to the elm:

If my sound advice you heed, if you follow where I lead,
You'll be healthy, you'll be strong and you'll be sleek;
You'll have muscles that are thick and a pretty little prick,
You'll be proud of your appearance and physique.

[ARISTOPHANES, *The Clouds* 1923; PP 153–4]

The speaker is a character in a comic play and is sending up the mannered ways of the intellectual élite of Athens, who probably had the same effect on the Athenian audience as the dons of Parson's Pleasure had on the students. As academies sprang up over the civilized world, their designers have rarely resisted a nod towards that original idea in the shape of a splashing fountain or cool green lawns and shady groves somewhere on the campus.

But if the Academy was romanticized, Arcadia was transformed out of recognition. It was, and it is, a remote and mountainous inland region of the Peloponnese, bare and barren. Its most famous son, the historian Polybius, describes it as lacking just about everything we associate with pastoral bliss. To him, Arcadia was a poor, waste, rocky, chilly country where the food that would grow was fit only for goats. The inhabitants had the reputation of being primitively musical – the god Pan was meant to inhabit the Arcadian mountain Maenalus – but they were a rough, unvarnished, unpoetical lot.

The Greek poet Theocritus is to blame for the appalling 'hey, nonny, nonny', 'nymphs and shepherds' school of bucolic versifying. He wrote his *Idylls* some time in the first half of the third century BC about the joys of country living and started off a flow of pastoral poetry around the world which hasn't yet quite dried up. Theocritus, being Greek, knew about Arcadia and was careful to set his pastoral scenes in Sicily which was better equipped for rustic rapture. But his shepherds and the goatherds spent their time tootling away to their loved ones on pan-pipes and so when Virgil, a foreigner unhampered by local knowledge, came to imitate Theocritus, he sited his rustic lovers in Arcadia because that was the home of Pan. And he went on to furnish the place with luxuriant vegetation, purling streams and unremitting leisure for love. The last quality is possibly the only one the area can fairly lay claim to, but when the Renaissance discovered Virgil the themes of his *Eclogues* were taken up with enthusiasm, and nymphs and shepherds have gambolled ever since about the verdant hills of an imaginary Arcadia in an idealized retreat from the pressures and complexities of city and court life.

Marlowe's *Passionate Shepherd* dwells in Arcadia; Shakespeare's *As You Like It* is set there, as is Spenser's *Shepherd's Calendar* and Milton's *Comus* and *Lycidas*. In music there are Bach's *Phoebus and Pan*. Debussy's *L'Après-midi d'un Faune*, Ravel's *Daphnis and Chloe* and Delibes' *Sylvia*. And in painting there is of course Poussin, with his enigmatic *Et in Arcadia Ego*, and the romanticized landscapes of Claude Lorraine, Watteau and Fragonard. The Arcadian series of Wedgwood pottery took the idyll to a wider audience. So Arcadia has had a long and successful run in Western Europe.

Just as Arcadia was romanticized into line with the ideals of a balmy pastoral scene dreamed by artists in the cloud-covered cities of northern Europe, so the culture of classical Greece was carefully shaped by the academics of northern Europe before being presented to us. Academics have a high regard for intellectual proficiency. After all they have it and it got them their jobs. So it is, perhaps, no coincidence that in Greek culture, which they identified as the cradle of civilization, academics found and admired those human qualities in which they were themselves proficient: intelligence, ingenuity, cleverness and rationality.

To the academics we owe all we know of classical Greece. And this includes those things which were so and those things which were not so. Without their patient investigations into the evolution of the language, the artefacts and buildings revealed by archaeology, the achievements of the Greeks would be hidden from us: but, as we have learned much from these scholars, we have also taken on board information based on their misconceptions.

Now, those of us who haven't spent the best years of our lives mastering the complexities of classical Greek and the literary and physical remains that enshrine the Greek heritage had better tread softly when it comes to questioning the judgements of those who have. But, at the risk of seeming impudent, and because, where academics squabble, those of us on the touchline can sometimes get a clearer view of the ball, I'd like to take a brief look at the origins of the view of Greece and the Greeks that kept me away from the place for half a century.

It seems likely that it originated in Germany during the eighteenth century. There was a feeling abroad that the Spirit of Civilization which had settled in Athens for a time and afterwards in Rome and the artistic centres of Renaissance Italy, was due for a spell in Germany. And German scholars applied themselves to classical studies with what they felt was a peculiar sympathy for the Greek genius. They were reacting against the undisciplined gaiety of the Rococo and wanted to replace the cynicism and flippancy of Watteau, Boucher and their ilk with a more puritanical morality and a stoic discipline in keeping with their national character. They felt that art should be purged of emotion, rationally constructed and morally improving.

The most influential of these German scholars was the son of a penniless cobbler from a small town, whose misconceptions were expressed with such rhapsodic fervour that they shaped the taste of several generations. Joachim Winckelmann wrote with passionate enthusiasm about the true nature of Greek art, which he saw as a demure, detached, almost glacial classicism producing figures of a tranquil beauty whose pulses never raced. He wrote that the Greeks studied to 'observe propriety both in feature and action' so that 'even a quick walk was opposed to their sense of decorum'.

Winckelmann thought of himself as unique in matters of artistic taste and judgement and an authority on the nude in life as well as in art. 'Nothing', he said, 'is more difficult to find in Nature than young men with beautiful knees' [quoted Honour 1973, p 117]. Although his ideas were challenged by the scholars of his day, he managed to persuade distinguished literary luminaries like Diderot and Madame de Stael that his notions of the essential Greek spirit were the right ones. He summarized that spirit in a famous phrase as *'eine edle Einfalt und eine stille Grosse'* (a noble simplicity and a calm grandeur).

Winckelmann was murdered by a petty thief before he managed to get to Greece and his ideas were formed by a prior conviction of what, in his perfect world, Greek art should represent – as confirmed by the many boring smooth white featureless copies that the Romans produced. His ideas were seized on by generations of classics masters with a sneaking if suppressed sympathy for Winckelmann's preoccupation with young men's knees and an open regard for the notion that the classicist should be rational, balanced, cool, morally uplifting and never out of breath.

They were able to keep up this mistaken idea of the essential Greek genius by carefully disegarding the evidence. Indeed, they were encouraged to do so by one of the great scholars of our own century, R. W. Livingstone:

Even in the greatest Greeks there is much that we must ignore. Supposing Plato and Pindar to have a vein of Orphism and Pythagoras queer on numbers; supposing Aeschylus to be touched with mysticism and Euripides with mysticism and morbidity, **the student of the Greek genius has a right to disregard these peculiarities.**

[LIVINGSTONE 1912; PP 25-6]

The bold italics are mine and they stress the important point here (we'll come to the details later in the book). If students are going to disregard what they think of as peculiarities of the Greek genius that are not to their taste, and if they pick up their taste from their tutors, it's no wonder that an academic tradition of what is essentially Greek is perpetuated in defiance of the evidence against it. One of Livingstone's contemporaries, a man of towering intelligence who could translate Greek into Latin shortly after he could walk and grew up to be Archbishop of Canterbury, was William Temple, who wrote of the classical Greeks:

The beauty which they express is, upon the whole, what we should call intellectual beauty; even in their sublimest moments they shrink from anything that suggests licence or lack or order. . . . This is, perhaps, because civilization was a thing so new, so precious and so permanently threatened both by the barbarism in the souls of the Greeks themselves, that they never really dared to let themselves go.   [TEMPLE 1916; PP 2-3]

The idea of the Greeks as a people who never really dared to let themselves go would split the sides of any Greek today. It could only have formed itself in the mind of a scholar who had applied himself with some care to disregarding those peculiarities which were not to the taste of an English cleric. But it helps perpetuate the academic tradition that the essential Greek genius was a cool, temperate rationality.

Before we look at the background to the real classical Greece, we might well ask why we should bother. Since there are other books to be read, other civilizations to be studied, other periods of history closer to our own, why turn the clock back quite so far?

It's worth listening to what one of the most famous Athenians thought worthwhile about the place when it was at its best:

We live under a system which does not copy the laws of our neighbours; it would be truer to say that we ourselves are a model for others than that we imitate anyone else. And its name — because the majority share in it and not just a few — is democracy. As far as the laws go, everyone is equal when settling private disputes; and as to the criteria by which anyone is picked out for public office, what matters is not his membership of a particular class but how distinguished he is in anything — his own personal qualities. Even being poor is no impediment; as long as he can be of value to the state, no man is barred from public life simply because poverty has made him obscure...

Further, we provide plenty of ways for the mind to refresh itself from business. We celebrate games and festivals all the year round and the elegance of our private establishments gives a daily delight which banishes gloom, while the size of the state draws the produce of the world into her harbour so that to the Athenian the fruits of other countries are as familiar a luxury as those of his own...

We cultivate refinement without extravagance and knowledge without effeminacy; wealth we employ more for use than for show and as for poverty — there's no disgrace in admitting it — the greater shame is in not taking steps to escape from it...

[Funeral speech of Pericles in THUCYDIDES II, 37; 40-1]

Of course the speech was no more a dispassionate analysis of the social situation than was the Gettysburg Address, but it makes claims about the way that society organized itself that are so closely in line with the ideals of our own, or of any time, that it seems worth asking how they came about and if they were realized.

Early History

Four thousand years ago, on the island of Crete, there was a powerful and rich civilization, so self-confident that it built its great palaces without fortifications of any kind. It seems to have been an aristocratic culture, under a king, with the title of *minos* — or some say that was his dynastic name – from which the civilization is called the Minoan. Its fleet ruled the Aegean and imposed tribute on far-off places. Possibly the myth of Theseus, who, by slaying the Minotaur, put an end to the Athenian annual tribute of men and girls to the palace at Knossos, is a record of this tribute. The palace itself, with its network of internal rooms, is certainly labyrinthine and easy to get lost in without a thread such as Ariadne provided. Today it still amazes because of its extensive sewerage system, including a flush toilet for the Queen. But as well as its excellent plumbing, the Minoan civilization produced vivid and vivacious paintings, exquisite carved gems, frescoes, furniture and necklaces to take the breath away. The second great pre-classical culture in Greece was that of the Mycenaeans, which flourished around the fourteenth to twelfth centuries BC. It was a blend of the Minoan with other invaders from the north; this civilization built palaces at Mycenae, Tiryns and Pylos in the Peloponnese and was the first to speak Greek. The Mycenean period was one of widespread magnificence. The wealth from commercial enterprise was accumulated in a long period of political stability and used to produce fine carvings in ivory, gold ornaments and precious stones of an astonishingly refined delicacy. The technical skills of the Myceneans were so advanced that the later Greeks thought their temples must be the work of the gods: the lintel across the door-posts of the Treasury of Atreus at Mycenae is a single block of stone that weighs 120 tons.

Homer

This is the time to meet Homer, because his poems were once thought to be set in the Mycenean age. We can deal with the big 'Homeric question' immediately by leaving it to somebody else. We don't know, nor does anybody, who or if Homer was. The Greeks thought they knew: he was their greatest poet, he was blind and he was born in one of the seven places that laid claim to the honour. And he composed both the *Iliad* and the *Odyssey*.

Now we know better and we know less. 'Homer was not written by Homer,' declared an examinee with modern insight, 'but by another man with the same name'. Sadly, even this may not be true; nineteenth-century German scholars beavered away at the texts to try to prove that the *Iliad* and the *Odyssey* weren't both written by the same person, or that they weren't both written by one man at all but possibly by a committee, and so far as I know there are American scholars feeding trillions of megabytes into huge computers in search of the answer.

It doesn't matter. We can read the books with delight without knowing a thing about their author(s). We get nothing extra out of *Hamlet* by knowing that Shakespeare was the third son of a butcher who left to his widow his second best bed.

So, to the great works themselves; at least, to confront the *Iliad* and the *Odyssey*. The biggest problem we have with these two is that they have been classics for centuries. Although Plato would have banished Homer from his republic, the poet was worshipped in antiquity. As early as the first century AD, the rhetorician Heraclitus recorded that:

From his tenderest years, the child just embarking on lessons is given Homer as a nurse for his unlicked mind; and what could be better than to let our imaginations feed on the milk of his poetry when we are scarce out of our swaddling clothes? As we grow, he always remains with us.   [QUOTED FLACELIERE 1965; P97]

He is reporting on a habit that had been in vogue for four centuries and which was revived in western Europe at the Renaissance. Everybody had to read Homer. And that meant the *Iliad* and the *Odyssey*. So they have long been accepted as established classics in the worst sense of the word; books to have on one's shelves, books to set in examination papers, books to have read, but which we never quite get around to reading. They don't deserve it because both are, in their different ways, far too enjoyable to have ended up as classics.

It is important to realize just how different they are. We make things much harder for ourselves, as first-time readers, if we approach them as a pair, like *Alice in Wonderland* and *Through the Looking Glass* or *Tom Sawyer* and *Huckleberry Finn*. This is a mistake. They are not a pair, even though they are both connected with the Trojan War. If we approach them with different expectations for each, we're more likely to get the best out of them. The *Iliad* is an epic poem. It deals with great events and great heroes tragically locked in a struggle for power, fame and honour. The *Odyssey* on the other hand is the world's first novel, a rattling good yarn with a psychology that's familiar to us, rounded characterization and cliff-hangers all the way.

The *Iliad* is a tougher read, and we need a mental adjustment before plunging in. If we approach it with the attitudes and values of our own time, we shall find it sonorous, bombastic and hollow. To come to terms with it we have to take on board the values of a heroic age, real or imagined. It is set in what anthropologists have called a 'shame culture' as opposed to a 'guilt culture'; that is one in which the main spur to human activity is the craving for public esteem and not the prickings of a private morality. It deals with people for whom honour, not virtue, is the greatest good; shame, not vice, the greatest evil. Kings were respected because they were powerful, not because they ruled with justice; they attracted loyalty by giving presents and not friendship. War was the most noble activity because through it came honour. The obligation to take revenge, especially for a killing, was absolute. The main characters in the *Iliad* find themselves inescapably having to do 'what a man's gotta do'.

This is well illustrated in the decision of Achilles, the central heroic figure of the *Iliad* who, as a child, was given the choice by his mother and decided that he would prefer a short life and a glorious death to a long and peaceful career in obscurity.

The poem opens in the ninth year of the ten-year siege of Troy, undertaken by the Greeks to bring back Menelaus' wife Helen, who left him for Paris, one of the sons of King Priam, and to avenge the honour of the Greeks. But Homer doesn't tell the whole story. He plunges straight in to the quarrel between Agamemnon, commander of the Greeks, and Achilles, one of his generals. The opening lines are amongst the most celebrated in all literature:

Sing, goddess, of the anger of Achilleus, son of Peleus, the accursed anger which brought uncounted anguish on the Achaians and hurled down to Hades many mighty souls of heroes, making their bodies the prey to dogs and birds' feasting; and this was the work of Zeus' will. [HOMER 1987; P 51]

But whatever our classics masters tell us about this being the magnificent opening of the great epic that is the cornerstone of western civilization, we have to admit that it doesn't really reach out and grab the unprepared reader. The book is not, at this point, I suggest, impossible to put down. If we are to press on with it, we need to know, as Homer's hearers knew, what point in the story of Troy he has chosen to focus on. The story can be quite simply told:

Agamemnon has given up a girl, a prize of war, and takes instead a girl belonging to Achilles who reacts by refusing to fight. Because Achilles is a great hero, things go badly for the Greeks and Agamemnon tries to make amends by apologizing and offering rich gifts, which Achilles refuses. But then the news comes that Patroclus, his dearest friend, has been killed by Hector and Achilles has to seek vengeance. He kills Hector before the walls of Troy and refuses to allow the body to be buried. Hector's father, the aged King Priam of Troy, pleads for the body and eventually Achilles, persuaded by his mother Thetis, gives it up. The poem ends with Hector's funeral.

The *Iliad* is a long poem. It can't be read at a sitting. It is violent; arms and heads are sliced off, brains are spattered around, blood spouts, teeth splinter. The battle descriptions are not for the squeamish:

Agamemnon stabbed him in the forehead with his sharp spear, and the heavy bronze of the helmet's rim could not stop the spear, but it went through that and through the bone, and all his brains were spattered inside. [IBID; P 197]

And there are sudden, short, striking images as when a soldier is shot through the breast:

He dropped his head to one side like a poppy in a garden, bent by the weight of its seed and the showers of spring; so his head drooped to one side under the weight of the helmet. [IBID; PP 159-60]

The great beauties of the poem are in its extended imagery. Often a striking fantasy seems to occur in the imagination of the poet who leaves the scene of the action for a time to pursue it and then returns to the impact of a short factual description. The vast army of the Trojans is camped on the plain at night:

As when the stars show brilliant in the sky around the shining moon, when the air is windless calm; all the hilltops and sharp headlands and mountain glens spring clear into sight, and brightness bursts infinite down from the sky; every star is seen and the shepherd's heart is glad. So many were the Trojans' fires burning clear in front of Ilios, between the ships and the stream of Xanthos. A thousand fires were burning in the plain, and round each there sat fifty men in the gleam of the blazing fire. And the horses stood beside their chariots munching their white barley and wheat and waiting for the throned dawn. [IBID; P 165]

There are many such beauties. The Iliad rewards the effort of reading but it is an uncompromisingly powerful tragedy. Great men fight and kill each other because a little man, Paris, a vain fop, has abused the hospitality of a Greek prince and run off with his wife to Troy. This is not a story of good men against bad, of right against might, but of great heroes on both sides dying for what seems to be a worthless cause.

The scene between Hector and his wife Andromache with their baby son is still poignant after two and a half thousand years. Andromache, in tears, takes Hector's hand:

Poor, dear man, your own brave spirit will destroy you, and you have no pity for your baby son and for me, your doomed wife, who will soon be your widow. Soon the Achaians will mass an attack on you and kill you. And for me, then, when I lose you, it would be better to sink down under the earth. There will be no other comfort left for me, when you meet your fate — only misery . . . [IBID; P 139]

Hector knows that what she says is true; that Troy will fall, that his brothers will be killed and that his wife will be carried off as a slave. But there is no choice:

I would feel terrible shame before the men of Troy and the women of Troy with their trailing dresses if like a coward I skulk away from the fighting. [IBID; P 139]

He is a hero and has to play the part whatever the consequences. He reaches forward to embrace his son:

But the child shrank back, crying against the breast of his girdled nurse, terrified at the sight of his own father, frightened by the bronze and the crest of horsehair as he saw it nodding dreadfully from the top of the helmet. His dear father and his honoured mother laughed aloud at this, and glorious Hector took the helmet straight from his head and laid it gleaming bright on the ground. Then he kissed his dear son and dandled him in his arms and said in a prayer to Zeus and the other gods: 'Zeus and you other gods, grant that this my son may become, as I have been, pre-eminent among the Trojans, as strong and brave as I ... May he carry home the bloody spoils of the enemy he has killed, and bring joy to his mother's heart.'   [IBID; P 140]

At such a moment, Hector can wish no more for his son than the honour that comes from killing and plunder. There is no other way to honour. Yet the manly heroes have a tenderness which makes them human. The great tragedy of the *Iliad* is that we are not faced with a struggle between good and evil: the good Greeks led by Achilles fighting the evil Trojans led by Hector. Achilles is too obsessed to be likeable and Hector too compassionate to be a villain. They have both the good and bad qualities of humans and they must fight, and one of them must die. Because the *Iliad* is not a romance, not a Western, in which the moral issues are clear-cut: it deals with all the ethical untidiness that confronts living people. It does not have the reassuring qualities of romantic fiction but the profoundly disturbing effects of great tragedy; if you read it you will be changed by it.

If you wanted to encourage your child's education in a fashionable 'undirective' way, there would be no point in leaving a copy of the *Iliad* around the house in the hope that it might be picked up, found immediately gripping, and read to the end. I've already mentioned my doubts about the opening. But with the *Odyssey* you stand a better chance. The plot if superb; it opens ten years after the fall of Troy when all the Greek survivors of the Trojan war have found their way home except Odysseus, who is on his way but has been delayed for seven years by the spell of the nymph Calypso. His wife Penelope waits patiently for him but, as the years go by, is more and more under pressure from a crowd of insolent suitors who have moved into the palace, are making free with the food and wine, and are competing with each other to slide into the absent king's bed and take over his kingdom. His son, Telemachus, it seems, can only wait, hoping for the day of his father's return when they will be slaughtered or driven from the palace. So, from the opening scene, we are caught up in anticipation of the possibility of a magnificent closing one.

The tension never slackens. We are told that Odysseus has offended the sea god Poseidon who is determined to prevent him from ever reaching home. And we know that there are many miles of sea to cross if he is ever to do so. But there is hope, because the goddess Athena is on his side. The Odyssey is the story of his adventures as he is helped and hindered on his long passage to his home, his palace, his queen and his vengeance on the suitors.

At the island of Aeaea, his men are entertained by the beautiful goddess Circe who prepares a feast for them:

... a mixture of cheese, barley meal, and yellow honey flavoured with Pramnian wine. But into this dish she introduced a noxious drug to make them lose all memory of their native land. And when they had emptied the bowls which she had handed them, she drove them with blows of a stick into the pig sties. Now, they had pigs' heads and bristles and they grunted like pigs; but their minds were as human as they had been before the change. So, weeping, they were penned in their sties. Then Circe flung them some forest nuts, acorns and cornelberries, the usual food of pigs that wallow in the mud.   [HOMER 1991; P 149]

Odysseus manages to rescue them, as he saved them from the one-eyed monster Cyclops and is to protect them against the charms of the Singing Sirens and brings them through the narrows between the sea monster Scylla and the whirlpool Charybdis. All these stories are better read than summarized, as is the conclusion, when, after losing twelve ships and nearly six hundred companions, Odysseus finally arrives on the shores of Ithaca and, disguised as a beggar, in the company of Eumaeus, a swineherd, approaches the palace. The swineherd warns Odysseus that he is in danger of being chased away by the suitors:

As they stood talking, a dog, lying there, lifted his head and pricked up his ears. Argus was his name. Odysseus himself had owned and trained him, though he had sailed for holy Ilium before he could reap the benefits. In years gone by the young huntsmen had often taken him *out after wild goats, deer and hares. But now, in his owner's absence, he lay abandoned on the heaps of dung from the mules and cattle that lay in profusion at the gate, awaiting removal by Odysseus' servants as manure for his great estate. There, full of vermin, lay Argus the hound. But, directly he became aware of Odysseus' presence, he wagged his tail and dropped his ears, though he lacked the strength now to come any closer to his master. Odysseus turned his eyes away and, making sure Eumaeus did not notice, brushed away a tear.*

[IBID; P 263]

The final chapter is breathtaking: no detail is spared to pile on the excitement as the great king, dressed as a beggar, is struck, abused and mocked by the suitors. Queen Penelope brings into the dining hall the great bow of Odysseus and twelve grey iron axes. She says that she will marry any man who can string the bow and shoot an arrow through each one of the iron axes. One by one the suitors try, but they are not strong enough to bend the bow. They fetch hot tallow and grease it but still the strongest of them can't bend it. Then the swineherd hands it to Odysseus and the suitors roar with laughter at the idea of the old tramp having the strength to string the bow ... The rest of the story may be predictable but it is magnificently told and must be read as Homer tells it.

We have met Homer during the Mycenean age because that is when he set his poems. Scholars have been quick to point out that he was writing hundreds of years later and that there are anachronisms – for example the iron axes in the bronze age – which show that he was less familiar with the Myceneans than we are today. Perhaps, in fact, the poems are set, not so much in a specific historical period – Homer was not a historian – as in an imagined age peopled by great warriors for whom courage and honour were the highest values, when the inevitability of human suffering could be put down to the interference of the gods. In such an age, unclouded by the petty and self-concerned perplexities of later times, great and pure tragedy is possible.

The Trojan War did, quite possibly, take place. There is evidence that the city which the excavators call Troy VIIA was violently destroyed. But in fact there was a series of Trojan wars which heralded the end of the Mycenean age. Suddenly, during the twelfth century,

15

the Myceneans disappear from archaeological digs. Their palaces were destroyed, their kings and people dispersed. The Dorians – so called because they settled in a place just north of the Corinthian Gulf called Doris – invaded from the north, but whether they drove out the Myceneans or occupied a vacuum created by other invaders is still uncertain. The period of time following these invasions has been called the Dark Ages. It was a time of culture clash and cultural assimilation out of which classical Greece was slowly to emerge.

Hesiod

We know very little about what went on in the Dark Ages. Homer, who was composing probably towards the end of the period, sings of the great deeds of the noblemen of an earlier time – either the Mycenean age or an imagined golden one – and this is what the aristocrats of his own time wanted to hear. But Hesiod, composing at about the same time, told them what they did not want to hear: about the corruption and exploitation they were guilty of in his day. He had personal experience of this: his brother had cheated him out of his fair share of their father's estate by bribing one of the local judges. He seems to have accepted this with the melancholy resignation of Eeyore, reflecting only that Zeus will eventually get around to punishing all crimes.

Hesiod hated the nobility but shared with them the feeling that the good old days were over. There had been, he writes, a golden age in the distant past when the earth put forth crops without the need of labour and men 'rich in flocks and dear to the blessed gods' lived in peace off the fields and died in their sleep without ever growing old. This was followed by an inferior silver age in which men were children for a hundred years but then grew up and 'lived in sorrow because of their foolishness.' They refused to worship the gods and so Zeus destroyed them and created a third race of bronze. Then men delighted only in war. They lived in bronze houses and killed each other with bronze weapons. The deterioration was halted for a time by 'a juster race and better', the heroes sung by Homer who found glory in the Trojan Wars and who 'with soul untouched of sorrow dwell in the islands of the blessed by the deep eddying Ocean; happy heroes for whom the bounteous earth bears honey-sweet fruit fresh twice a year'. The fifth race of men, amongst whom Hesiod lived, were envious, brawling, of hateful countenance. And the young people had no respect for their parents.

Hesiod hated women, the upper classes and the weather. But, although he is a doleful figure, you get the feeling when reading him that you are being offered an unvarnished picture of the times. He was never one to gloss over difficulties. His own smallholding on the northern slopes of Mount Helicon he describes as 'Askra, awful in winter, miserable in summer, and no good at any time'.

His longest surviving poem is the *Theogony*, which has been well described as 'a list of who slept with whom on Mount Olympus, a sort of eighth-century *Dallas*' [Leckie 1989; pxxxix]. It's not an easy read, having the literary charm of the opening of St Matthew's Gospel – the begatting bit – and is mainly useful as a source book for chroniclers of Greek myth. Far more accessible is his poem *Works and Days*, in which he sets out, in 828 hexameters, practical advice on farming techniques. This anticipates by about 2700 years the BBC serial *The Archers*, in that it sets out to be agriculturally informative and entertaining at the same time. And it works. The plot is based on the quarrel Hesiod had with his brother Perses over the loss of the estate. He tried to end the feud by offering free agricultural advice. To everything there is a season, and Hesiod spells them out; when the crane first cries, it is the signal for winter ploughing; when Orion rises, the chaff should be winnowed from the grain and:

When the Pleiades fleeing before the fearful strength of Orion plunge into the misty sea then the blast of all the winds rages; at that time keep ships no more on the wine-dark sea, but remember and till the soil as I tell you. Draw up your ship on land and prop it with stones on all sides to withstand the power of the wet blasts of the winds; and pull out the sea plug so that the storm-rain of Zeus does not rot it. [HESIOD 1908; P 23]

The poem is packed with wise saws about the good life as well as practical agricultural advice; people who gossip will themselves be the subject of tattle; barns should be built in the summer and not at time of harvest; a man should marry at the age of thirty, choosing as a wife a girl of sixteen who is then young enough to be taught good habits; she should be from the local neighbourhood. 'Try, if you can, to have an only son, to care for the family inheritance; that is the way wealth multiplies in one's halls.'

The poem ends with the words:

Blessed and happy he who knows all these things and works unblamed by the immortals judging the flight of birds and avoiding sins.   [IBID]

There is an irony in the story that Hesiod, who had spent his years preaching hard work and an upright life, was killed by two brothers he was visiting in Locris, on the ground that he had seduced their sister.

The Polis

At the end of the Dark Ages we can see a great change in society. The kings and the kingdoms have vanished and in their place are hundreds of small independent political units which form the base of Greek culture in her greatest years. They were each called the 'polis', a word often translated as 'city-state', but since that phrase seems to imply that a city ruled a country, it is inaccurate. We have to tackle the polis at this stage because, without having a clear idea of what it was and what it meant to the Greeks, 'it is quite impossible to understand properly Greek history, the Greek mind, or the Greek achievement' [Kitto 1951; p 65].

I might as well come clean and admit that politics has never been a strong suit with me. In political discussions I have to work hard, not to maintain an interest but to stay awake. I use party political broadcasts to get over bouts of insomnia. I don't defend this attitude but feel I must admit it to a reader who has been good enough to stay with me so far. If Man, as Aristotle said, is a 'political animal', then it always seemed to me that I must be a biological sport.

But, just in case there is anybody else out there whose eyes glaze over in political discussions, I have some encouraging news. Aristotle's phrase is often bandied about by party activists as if those of us with a healthy apathy to the subject were abnormal; as if people matured into card-carrying Young Conservatives or Socialist Workers by a process of biological development; as if a passion for politics should naturally grow with hair on the chin and the sexual appetite.

But I'm delighted to discover that it's the young activists who have it wrong. Aristotle did indeed say that Man is a political animal, but he didn't mean that man is biologically programmed to join political parties; he meant simply that man is naturally drawn to living in a polis. And he explained why:

First of all, it is inevitable that those who cannot live without each other will form a union. Male and female do so, for instance, to reproduce the species – not from conscious choice, this, but from a natural instinct common to all animals and plants, to leave behind something akin to themselves ... the natural unit to meet all man's daily needs is thus the household ... Then when a number of households are first united for the satisfaction of something more than day-to-day needs, the result is the village ...

Finally the ultimate partnership, made up of numbers of villages and having attained the height, one might say, of self-sufficiency – this is the polis. It has come into being in order, simply, that life can go on; but it now exists so as to make that life a good life ... So, from all this it is evident that the polis exists by natural processes, and that it is natural for man to live in a polis. [ARISTOTLE, Politics, 1252a2hh]

That last phrase is the one so often mistranslated as 'man is a political animal'. In its context you can see that it means nothing of the kind.

Aristotle's explanation of the evolution of the polis is as good as any other, although many historians have explained it as the natural result of Greece being broken up into so many small independent geographical units; mountain valleys or islands. The problem with this explanation is that so many areas which were not physically broken up were still divided into small political units and many of the mountainous districts never developed *poleis* (the plural of *polis*) at all. Also, when the Greeks set up colonies abroad, they took with them this form of political organization. So, it seems, they just liked to live this way.

This is understandable when you realize that the polis was large enough to be economically self-sufficient, but small enough for everybody to know everybody else – there were exceptions, Athens having around 250 000 people in the fifth century. The polis had a centre for civic and religious buildings where the citizens could assemble to discuss the running of the place, and usually an acropolis – a high place which could be fortified and used as a citadel in time of war. The surrounding countryside was part of the polis in that it shared the myths and traditions and its people took part in the government of the place and in its religious ceremonies. The poleis did vary a lot in size. Athens, the largest of them, was about 2600 square kilometres (1000 square miles) in all, whereas the island of Ceos, which is only about a third of the size of ancient Athens, was divided into four small poleis, which means it could have had four governments running four armies being paid in four different currencies and operating four different calendars. So we can think of the polis, not so much as a place but as a community of people who acted in concert. Official documents always speak of 'The Athenians' rather than 'Athens'.

We'll hear more about the organization of the polis when we come to talk about democracy in a later chapter. For now, it's helpful to know that, when we hear about Sparta or Thebes or Athens, we're not to have in mind great cities or even hilltop towns, but bodies of people who lived in an area with an administrative centre and who were united by having their own laws, coinage, customs, festivals and religious rites. The history of Greece is the history of these poleis, of which the most influential and famous were Sparta and Athens.

Sparta

I first came across Sparta in the Boy Scouts. Many of us did. One of the Scouts' laws says 'A scout smiles and whistles under all difficulties.' To explain what this means, we were told the story of the Spartan lad and the fox cub as an example of behaviour to which, as Boy Scouts, we could aspire – though it's a bit of an oddity as a moral tale.

The Spartan lad, you remember, had stolen a fox cub and hidden it under his tunic when he was caught and brought before the magistrate on a charge. He steadily denied all knowledge of the crime and was put under severe cross-examination, protesting all the while his innocence. And then suddenly the lad fell down dead. The fox cub had bitten through his clothes and had been eating into his guts all the time and the lad was smiling and keeping his cool and, for all we know, whistling. It was a fine example of fortitude and endurance − of true grit. Alongside the Spartan lad, George Washington comes over as something of a wet in that business of the cherry tree. He, of course, couldn't tell a lie, whereas our hero refused to speak the truth: an odd hero, when you think about it, for the Boy Scouts.

The Spartans have managed, over three thousand years or so, to kindle admiration amongst the most unlikely personalities from Nietzsche to Lord Baden-Powell. Yet they were a rum lot. The first thing to say is that we probably know a lot less about them than we think we do. This is because they were always very secretive. For centuries they kept a closed society, rather like communist Russia or red China, and they periodically expelled foreigners who had settled there. They wrote nothing about themselves from the sixth century BC − they weren't given to literary pursuits − and those who did write about them tended to be ideological admirers, rather like the visitors to Russia or China in the palmy days of communism who would write glowing reports of how much better they ordered things over there. There is also, I sense, a problem with our academics who seem to be temperamentally either for or against the Spartans. Roughly speaking, if you feel that the youth of today need more understanding and compassion you're likely to be against the Spartans, but if you're all for military service and bringing back the cat to make them shape up, you'll find Sparta to your taste.

The Spartans were Dorians who settled in the Peloponnese and kept themselves apart from the natives. They had a strong sense of superiority and were a very closely knit and traditional community. Some time in the eighth century, five of their villages in the great plain of Laconia combined and, needing more land for settlement, simply spread out, conquered all the inhabitants and gave them a new and inferior status of *perioikoi*, which means something like 'neighbours'. These were denied Spartan citizenship but paid taxes, were liable for military service and produced goods and services for the Spartans.

As their population expanded, the Spartans, being a rather stolid and centripetal folk, didn't solve the problem by going off and founding colonies elsewhere, as many poleis did. They simply expanded into the neighbouring plain of Messenia and reduced the inhabitants to the status of *helots*, or serfs, whose lives were nasty and brutish. This was a comfortable enough arrangement for the Spartans, supported as they were by the forced labour of a conquered people, but it had a snag: surrounded by a hostile and resentful population which outnumbered them about twenty to one, they could never really relax and enjoy themselves. They were always having to set off and suppress rebellions. In fact, it's easy to get the impression that the Spartans were incapable of enjoying themselves, which may be one reason why they are so admired by those with a mission to improve us.

The chief duty of a mounted policeman, as I was once told by a communist party official in Poland, is to stay in the saddle. And the Spartans organized their society from birth to death with this as their main objective. Being unable to convince the helots that they were better off as slaves, the Spartans had to keep them in order by military force and so their society was an army on continual active service. This meant that every citizen had to be fit to fight and every Spartan baby boy was presented to a board of elders for a decision on whether or not he should be allowed to live. If weak or malformed, he was tossed into a ravine. If allowed to live, his education was entirely organized by the State. 'Education' isn't quite the right word, with its connotations of expansion or leading out of the understanding. Training is better. The boys were regimented from the age of eight into hierarchically organized groups according to age. From eight to eleven they were called *robidas*, which means something like 'wolf cub'. They were divided into bands under the command of older adolescents and subdivided into patrols each under the command of the brightest boy. From twelve to their fifteenth birthday, they were boys, and from sixteen to twenty they were *eiren*, divided into grades from the first to the fifth year. The similarity with our Cubs and Scouts has been exaggerated: these lads could not go home to Mum when the weekend camp was over. Hitler Youth comes closer.

The object of the training was to develop military skills and a sense of group loyalty. Battles were organized between different classes of the same age group in which clemency was not encouraged. A pile of cheeses would be set in front of the altar of Artemis and one group given the task of seizing it against the defences of another group armed with whips; the younger boys were made to stand nude for long periods at the hottest time of the day to test their endurance. Their heads were shaved and they were fed rather less food than they needed to encourage them to steal. Stealing showed enterprise and so was a good thing; being caught demonstrated stupidity and was severely punished. As the boys graduated to the élite of the *eiren* classes, they were put through initiation ceremonies and made to live alone in the wildest countryside, concealed from search parties, like the *lykanthropos*, or werewolf. They were given the task of hunting down the helots and even, it has been said, killing one of them as proof of manhood.

... they neither would, nor could live alone, but were in manner as men incorporated one with another, and were always in company together, as the bees be about their master bee: still in a continual love to serve their country, to win honour, and to advance the common weal. [PLUTARCH, *Lycurgus* 253]

Many other societies have put their youth through initiation rites, separation from the family and military training; but Sparta was unique in that the clear aim of the training was the total suppression of individuality in the young and the instilling of a lifelong commitment to the State.

Even the grown men were organized. Until his thirtieth year, a Spartan male slept in the dormitories he had grown used to. He could marry, but family relationships were discouraged as being likely to give rise to loyalties that might compete with the State. He shouldn't even be seen going to or coming from his wife. Some suggest that this was because stronger children were produced by couples who really lusted after each other and could only come together by stealth, rather than those conceived in the satiated somnolence of a marriage bed. But it could have been simply that the Spartans would never do anything openly if it was possible to arrange for it to be achieved by cunning.

The adult males were also obliged to dine together, rather like barristers of the Inns of Court, and for the same reasons: to consolidate the society and preserve its traditions. The ambience of the mess in Sparta differed from that in Chancery Lane: the historian Xenophon tells us that the conversation there revolved around noble deeds with 'little or no insolence, little or no drunkenness and little or no indecency in behaviour and talk'. Certainly the menu was more of a challenge: the meals tended to culminate in the infamous 'black broth' of Sparta, a vile concoction of unitemised but unspeakable ingredients which only the most intrepid could face. The nonchalance of Spartan soldiers when faced by certain death on the battle field has been put down to the fact that this was at least one way of getting away from the food.

There were, of course, no dancing girls on hand, no fine tableware or lordly dishes. The Spartans were very high-minded about luxuries of any kind. There was also a practical reason for their having to go without foreign goods and bric-à-brac: they had no money. Or, at least, they had no gold and silver coinage, but made do with the old-fashioned iron bars as a medium of exchange. This had the advantage that nobody would steal it or accept it as a bribe – the bars had been quenched when red-hot by pouring vinegar on to them which left them brittle and unworkable so they couldn't even be cut up and used for something. Nobody would load up the stuff and cart it into the rest of Greece where, in any case, it was seen as worthless and ludicrous. So there were no foreign luxuries available in Sparta, but the craftsmanship of their couches, chairs and tables was sound. An item particularly valued, especially on military campaigns, was the Spartan drinking cup because, as Plutarch reports,

... its colour concealed the unpleasant appearance of the water that soldiers are obliged to drink, while its inward-curving rim kept the foul sediment back inside and allowed only the purer part to fill the drinker's mouth.   [PLUTARCH *Lycurgus* 9.4]

The Spartan drinking cup is a fitting symbol of their austere way of life. The ideology behind it inspired the more rigorous of British public schools, especially those which placed character above learning. It has been well expressed by Thucydides, in the words he put into the mouth of the Spartan King Archidamus:

Because of our well-ordered life we are both brave in war and wise in council. Brave because self control is based upon a sense of honour, and honour is based on courage. And we are wise because we are not so highly educated as to look down upon our laws and customs, and are too vigorously trained in self control to be able to disobey them.

[THUCYDIDES 1972; P 85]

Athens

In contrast with Sparta, Athens was to encourage education to the point when its citizens did look down on their laws and customs. But the side benefits were considerable.

When, in the years leading up to 600 BC, Sparta was making itself the greatest power in the Peloponnese and, for that matter, in the whole of Greece, Athens was a small and insignificant town. The territory of Attica, which surrounds the city, was populated by small farmers under independent local aristocratic lords who spent their time squabbling for power. Gradually they came to accept that stability came from wider loyalties and they began to focus on one family in one place: Athens. Traditionally it was Theseus who unified Attica and his descendants ruled in Athens as kings.

An important stage in the unity and development of any community is the acquisition of laws. No matter how severe the laws are, at least they are predictable, unlike the whims of the aristocracy, so we must assume that the Athenians reacted with some relief when, in 621, the first code of laws was defined and published – even though their author was a man called Draco. The most common penalty, even for minor infringements, was death. When Draco was asked how he could justify this, he said he quite saw the problem but law-breakers should obviously be put to death and he regretted that he had been unable to think up a more severe penalty for the serious offenders.

Even when the peasants of Attica were given a code of laws, they continued to have problems with the land tenure system which made them pay a sixth of their produce to the landowners and left them open to being enslaved for non-payment of debts. They were liberated by the first historical hero of Athens, Solon. He was a merchant, a traveller, a philosopher and a poet. When he wrote about the injustices of life being caused by human greed, the population of Athens did not react by hailing him as a revolutionary folk hero; they more sensibly gave him the powers of a dictator and told him to put things right. This he tried to do by reducing debts, restoring lands which had been lost to creditors, and substituting a property qualification for the birth qualification which had kept the government of the city in the hands of a few noble families. He divided the citizens into classes based on their income which was expressed in terms of bushels of produce. The highest class were the 'five hundred bushel men' who were eligible for election to the highest offices. As a further encouragement to social stability, Solon ordained that every father must teach his son a trade.

Having put all these reforms into place, Solon resigned the dictatorship so that he would not become the focus of a personality cult. He once told a friend that tyranny was a high place from which there was no easy way down. So he set off again on his travels, warning the Athenians to place their trust in laws and not in men. He left a poetic record of what he thought he had managed to achieve:

To the people I have given privilege enough,
Neither taking away nor adding to their status.
Those who had power and were famed for their wealth
I took care equally not to injure.
I stood firm, holding my strong shield over both
And did not allow either side to triumph unjustly.   [SOLON FR. 5]

When the strong shield was removed, the squabbling began again, not so much between the classes as amongst the aristocracy, jealous for power. It ended with one of them, Peisistratus, taking over control of Athens as a tyrant. At the time, the word 'tyrant' was not pejorative; it meant simply someone who had come to power by non-constitutional means. Peisistratus was an enlightened despot. He redistributed land amongst the peasants, handing out much that had been confiscated. He was himself a country landowner by origin and knew the value of keeping on good terms with his tenants. He taxed their produce and one day, a story goes, visited a poor farmer on an arid patch of land to ask how much he got out of it. The man, not recognizing him, said all he got was aches and pains and he wished Peisistratus would take his ten per cent of them. The story goes on to record that Peisistratus laughed and made him exempt from all taxes.

The taxes were needed for civic works: Peisistratus constructed a fountainhouse in Athens to bring water into Athens, rebuilt the city, encouraged the arts of sculpture and vase painting and organized both the national festivals of Dionysus at which dramas were performed and the Panathenaic Festivals at which recitals of Homer were given. But it is the way of despotism that the benevolence does not outlast a generation. There is a story that Peisistratus once reprimanded one of his sons for arrogant behaviour to a citizen: 'I don't behave like that.' 'Ah, but you didn't have a tyrant for a father.' 'No, and if you behave like that you won't have a tyrant for a son.'

He was right. His son ruled so harshly that the population rose against him and, with the help of Sparta, drove him and his family out of Athens. The way was clear for the third great name which even the most potted history of Athens must contain: Cleisthenes, the founder of Athenian democracy.

The power of the nobility, which had caused so much instability in Athens, was enshrined in the system which allowed four 'tribes', or groups of noble families, to elect the archons – the holders of the highest office in the state. This meant that the heads of the groups of families were certain to be elected. Cleisthenes had the imagination and courage to recreate Athenian society by dividing it into ten new 'tribes', based on residence rather than birth – though each was allowed to fabricate its instant traditions and ancestors – each of which was composed of a roughly equal number of parishes. The important new idea was that Attica was divided into three areas: city, inland, and coast, and that each of the ten tribes contained parishes from each of the three divisions. So the citizen's political identity was based on where he lived and no longer on his membership of related families. Cross-sections of the population with conflicting interests to be reconciled belonged to these new tribes. Each tribe chose fifty names by lot to belong to a council of 500 where the real political decisions were taken. The power of the ancient families had been replaced by the closest approximation to a democracy that had yet evolved in the history of mankind.

Persia Looks West

Greeks from central Greece had settled in Ionia, the coast of Asia Minor, from the tenth century and had built substantial cities there which by the sixth century were prospering as independent political units in the territory of the King of Lydia. In 560, that throne was occupied by Croesus, the proverbially moneyed monarch who has a place in Greek history because, like so many others, he misunderstood the words of the oracle at Delphi. Having an eye on the neighbouring territory of Media, then ruled by the Persian King Cyrus the Great, first King of the Medes and Persians, whose empire stretched from India to the Black Sea, Croesus asked the oracle if he should cross the River Halys, the boundary between them, and invade. The oracle replied that, if he crossed the river, he would destroy a great empire. Encouraged by these words, he did so. The oracle proved right: but the empire he destroyed by crossing the river was his own.

Cyrus conquered Lydia and so, by 548, the Persian power was on the shores of the Aegean. When Cyrus's son Cambyses added Egypt to the Persian Empire and his successor Darius invaded the lands north of the Danube, the Greek Ionian cities were on the fringes of the greatest empire the world had ever known. They were governed from

Sardis, the former capital of Lydia, which became the seat of the local Persian satrap, or provincial governor.

The Persians pushed further into Greece, but at a gentle pace, Darius invading Thrace and Macedonia in 512. The Greeks along the coast of Ionia, who had exchanged one master for another, seemed contented enough until the year 499, which is the first date to try to remember, when they rose in revolt with the help of twenty ships from Athens and eight from Eretria and burned the Persian capital of Sardis. The revolt went on for five years but collapsed in 494, when the Persians sacked Miletus. Darius was so irritated by the whole business that he decided that he must get around to conquering Greece one day and had a servant whisper to him each evening at his meal 'Remember the Athenians'.

Herodotus

The Persian Wars are our chance to meet one of the most captivating personalities of the time: Herodotus, the Father of History. He was the first to write a history of the period and will be an engaging companion as we travel through it. Herodotus usually comes with a health warning: he was not over-sceptical about his sources and is often represented by modern historians as naive and credulous.

Now, I did a stretch as a professional historian, by which I mean I was paid by a university to research and write about what happened in the past. At least, that's what I thought when I took the job. But I soon found out that historians make their reputations, not by writing about what happened in the past but by discovering and making public the mistakes of other historians. In fact, there's a piece of advice that gets bandied about amongst the beginners: 'Never go into a field of research unless a fool has been there before you'. You can then make a name by pointing out his follies.

Herodotus would have been astonished that his descendants spent their time squabbling in this way. For him, history carried the meaning of the Greek word *istoria*, which means 'enquiry' or 'investigation'. And the 'history' he wrote is simply a record of his enquiries, a sort of interim report which makes no claim to infallibility, only to readability, where it scores high. If Herodotus was given an explanation of why something happened, he would record it for the amusement of his readers and leave it up to them to form a judgement as to its probability. 'My job', he wrote, 'is to write what has been said, but I do not have to believe it' [quoted Grant 1989; p 79]. Sometimes, if he heard two different versions, he would record them both and the reader could decide between them. And he wasn't afraid to introduce a personal note of scepticism occasionally. When he reports that the people of Thessaly believe that a river gorge was caused by the god Poseidon, he goes on: 'anyone who believes that Poseidon shakes the earth and the chasms caused by earthquake are the work of that god would say, if he saw this one, that Poseidon made it; but it seems to me that the parting of the mountains was caused by an earthquake.' The fleet of Xerxes was destroyed by a great storm. Herodotus writes:

The storm lasted three days, after which the Magi brought it to an end by sacrificial offerings, and by putting spells on the wind ... or, of course, it may be that the wind just dropped naturally.   [HERODOTUS 1972; p 508]

So he wasn't completely naive; but he was curious about everything and wandered off into long digressions about the source of the Nile, the habits of the hippopotamus and the crocodile and the sexual customs of African tribes.

Herodotus wrote that his aim was to trace the events which brought Greece into conflict, with a full description of that memorable struggle; we can now, in his company, follow the great wars that took place between Europe and Asia. To taste the flavour of Herodotus, it's worth a brief backward glance at the coming to power of the Persian Emperor Darius the Great, King of Kings, Lord of the Civilized World in Asia and Africa. He tells the story that, on the death of Cambyses, the six noblemen who were competing to replace him agreed to a bizarre method of selection. They would all mount their horses before dawn and the rider of the first horse to whinny as the sun rose would be king. Darius had an ingenious groom called Oebares who told him his election was in the bag:

Oebares, as soon as it was dark, took from the stables the mare which Darius' horse was particularly fond of, and tied her up on the outskirts of the city. Then he brought along the stallion and led him round and round the mare, getting closer and closer in narrowing circles, and finally allowed him to mount her. Next morning, just before dawn, the six men, according to their agreement, came riding through the suburbs of the city and when they reached the spot where the mare had been tethered the previous night, Darius' horse started forward and neighed. At the same instant, although the sky was clear, there was a flash of lightning and a clap of thunder . . . [IBID; PP 241-2]

After his election, Darius, according to Herodotus, put up a stone relief in memory of this occasion. It showed a man on horseback and an inscription which read: 'Darius son of Hystaspes, by the virtue of his horse and of his groom Oebares gained the throne of Persia.'

The First Persian Invasion

In 490, the army of Darius crossed the Aegean and attacked Eretria. Darius himself stayed at home since the conquest of Greece was a small matter and clearly shouldn't take long. After a siege of seven days Eretria was taken and burned to the ground. Then the Persian ships and army crossed to the nearest landing point on the mainland which happened to be a place called Marathon. News of the landing was carried to the king of Sparta by the first Marathon runner, Pheidippides, with a call for help. But the Spartans were busy with a religious festival and arrived too late for the battle.

Nobody is quite sure how many Persians faced the Athenian infantry of 10 000, plus about 600 Plataeans. Anecdote has added to their number, but it seems likely to have been about 15–20 000 infantry, cavalry and archers. They were representative of the most powerful empire on earth and they wore trousers, which unsettled the beskirted Greeks. In order to extend his battle line to the same length as the Persians, the Greek general Miltiades thinned the centre and when, at dawn one day in early September, the Athenians charged across the plain at the enemy, the Persians easily broke through that vulnerable centre. But the Greeks then wheeled inwards and engulfed the Persians.

As the broken army fled towards the sea and their waiting ships, the Persians left 6400 dead on the battlefield of Marathon, together with 192 Athenians. It was one of the most famous victories of all time. The middle-class Greek citizens of an unmilitary state had shown that the great army of the Persian Empire was not invincible. A painting of the battle was set up in a public portico in Athens and the dead of Marathon were buried in a great mound which is still visited with respect today.

After Marathon there was a respite of ten years during which the Persians were preoccupied with a revolt in Egypt and finding a replacement for Darius, who died in 486. The Athenians were given a bonus at this time by the discovery of a new and rich vein of silver in the mines at Mount Laurium. Public finances were simple affairs in those days and the citizens proposed that the money should be divided amongst them, but Themistocles, who became the first non-aristocrat to direct the affairs of state, persuaded them to spend the money on 200 warships. The fleet was built just in time.

The Second Persian Invasion

In 480 came the second Persian invasion, led by the King Xerxes. This time the army was too large to transport by sea, though it was unlikely to have reached the five million that Herodotus reports. 'There was not a nation in all Asia,' he writes 'that he did not take with him against Greece; save for the great rivers there was not a stream his army drank from that was not drunk dry.' Xerxes himself directed operations so that there would be no humiliation this time for the mighty emperor. He built a bridge across the Hellespont from Asia to Europe but, just before the mighty army could cross, a storm rose and the waves smashed up the bridge and carried it away. Xerxes, Great King and Lord of the Civilized World, etc., was unused to being crossed, even by the sea, and he

gave orders that the Hellespont should receive three hundred lashes and have a pair of fetters thrown into it. And I have heard before now that he also sent people to brand it with hot irons. [HERODOTUS 1972; P 249]

The bridge was rebuilt; the great army crossed and passed slowly through Thrace and Macedonia, then turned south towards Athens, the fleet following along the coast.

This time the Greeks rallied around Sparta and a famous stand was taken at the pass of Thermopylae. Here Xerxes sent a spy to count the numbers of the Greeks. When he learned how few were there, he waited for four days for them to surrender, unable to believe that they would dare to oppose his multitude. But the spy reported that the Spartan soldiers spent the time oiling their bodies and combing their long hair, with no sign of concern about the approaching battle. The story is reported by Herodotus that when the Spartan Dieneces was told the Persians were so numerous that when their archers shot, the arrows hid the sun, he replied: 'This is pleasant news ... for if the Persians hide the sun, we shall have our battle in the shade.'

Three hundred Spartans, led by their king, Leonidas, held back the entire Persian army for a week. Finally, when a traitor had shown the Persians a track by which they could be surrounded, the Spartans were slaughtered, those who had lost their swords fighting on with fists and teeth. A monument at that place still bears the words:

Stranger, go tell the Spartans that we lie here
Obedient to their laws.

As the Persians swept south, the Athenians retreated to the island of Salamis, just off the coast opposite Athens where they could see the Persians burning their houses and tearing down the temples on the Acropolis. The oracle had told the Athenians to 'put their trust in the wooden wall' which Themistocles interpreted as meaning the Athenian fleet and fortunately he got it right: when the Persian ships were lured into the narrow channel between Salamis and the mainland, they were crushed by the Athenians.

The defeat had been observed by Xerxes, who had taken up a

position on a vantage point to enjoy the inevitable Persian victory. Byron was to tell the tale with some satisfaction:

The king sate on the rocky brow
Which looks o'er sea-born Salamis;
And ships, by thousands, lay below,
And men in nations — all were his!
He counted them at break of day —
And when the sun set, where were they?
[Don Juan, canto III, stanza 86, 4]

Xerxes decided that, having burned Athens, which was what he had set out to do, he could reasonably return home and did so, leaving 300 000 men with his son-in-law Mardonius who wanted to fight a final battle to regain the honour of the great Empire. It was fought the following year at Plataea, in Boeotia:

The armies engaged first in a struggle for the barricade of shields; then, the barricade down, there was a bitter and protracted fight, hand to hand, close by the temple of Demeter. Again and again the Persians would lay hold of the Spartan spears and break them; in courage and strength they were as good as their adversaries, but they were deficient in armour, untrained and greatly inferior in skill ... They pressed hardest at the point where Mardonius fought in person — riding his white charger — and surrounded by his thousand Persian troops, the flower of the army. While Mardonius was alive, they continued to resist and to defend themselves ... but after his death and the destruction of his personal guard, the finest of the Persian troops, the remainder yielded to the Lacedaemonians and took to flight.   [HERODOTUS 1972; P 577]

The great invasion was over; Asia was in retreat; Greek civilization had triumphed over oriental barbarism.

The Delian League

The victory of the Greeks over the Persians confirmed them in their view of themselves as, by nature and nurture, superior to all barbarians. As Athens was rebuilt, the temple pediments were sculpted to show the earth-born giants being crushed by the gods of Olympus. Athenian trade and industry prospered and the potters and painters, the architects and sculptors brought their arts to a new level of perfection. To guard against another Persian invasion, the Athenians organized a league of the states most likely to be under threat. Over 150 of them joined, from Thrace, the islands of the Aegean and the Ionian cities of Asia Minor. They all contributed money, ships and manpower to keep the Aegean free from pirates and from Persians. The league's headquarters and treasury were on the island of Delos, sacred to Apollo.

Sparta didn't join. The threat from Persia was mainly to the coast of Ionia and the islands of the Aegean; pirates were not a problem to an agricultural economy; and the League needed ships, which meant the Athenian fleet. Athens as the original home of the Ionians was ideologically right to lead the League to protect them. One of the League's first actions was to conquer the island of Skyros and plant an Athenian military outpost there. This protected the main sea lane from the Black Sea to Athens and also allowed the Athenians to bring back from Skyros the remains of Theseus, legendary founder of the city, for ceremonial reburial in Attica. It was already clear that the money and ships of the Delian League were considered by Athens to be at her disposal.

The League, which had begun as an alliance, soon became an Athenian Empire. When the island of Naxos wanted to drop out, protesting that the Persian threat no longer existed, they were crushed by the league's forces and a heavy payment was imposed on them. When the headquarters of the League, and its treasury, were moved to Athens it could have been argued that the money was safer in the Acropolis than on a small and exposed island, but the move was seen as yet another sign that the Athenians thought of it as theirs. When funds were taken from the League's treasury to rebuild the temples of Athens and to pay its citizens for public service, there were protests from members of the League. But a powerful statesman with an imperialist cast of mind was in charge and he replied simply that they were paying for the protection of the Athenian fleet and they were getting it. The buildings and statues which demonstrated the power of Athens added to the greater glory of Greece.

Pericles

The man whose name has been given to the greatest age of human achievement in the history of the world would not have been a bit surprised. Pericles was a well-born, aloof, majestic character who never smiled and is said to have wept only twice in his life. He was a democrat without the common touch. He rarely spoke in public meetings, but when he did so his manner and his delivery were described as 'Olympian'. Democracy meant, for him, not so much the untrammelled power of the people to control events, which he would have thought simple-minded, but the equality of all before the law. The common people of Athens admired him and he arranged for them to be, for the first time, paid for public services like jury duty and also for the poorer among them to get into the theatre without paying. It didn't take long for the handouts to undermine the slender appetite for work of the poorer classes — at least in the view of the well-off: Plato wrote that they made the Athenians 'idle, cowardly, garrulous and grasping' [quoted Grant 1989; p 69]. But the vast programme of public works not only beautified Athens, it gave employment to all.

The Athenians, for all their zest for life and undeniable achievements, were not comfortable characters to be with. On a desert island, or for a weekend in the country, one would seek other companions. Not only did they see life as an *agon*, a struggle in which the best men always won, they seem to have felt it a social or political duty to stir up everybody else. There's a description of the Athenians' character in Thucydides:

If some project of theirs is a failure, they compensate themselves with hopeful plans of some other sort: for what is unique about them and their plans is that hoping for something amounts to the same as possessing it, so quickly do they put into effect whatever they have decided to do. And so they toil on, through hardships and dangers all their lives — deriving little or no pleasure from what they already have done because they are perpetually adding to it. Their only idea of a holiday is to do what needs doing, and they respond to peace and quiet more badly than to hard labour. Consequently, one would best describe them, in a nutshell, as men congenitally incapable either of living a quiet life themselves or of allowing the rest of humanity to do so.   [THUCYDIDES 1.70]

Peloponnesian Wars _____

The rise of Athens to power was resented but eventually tolerated by the members of the Delian League; Sparta saw it as a threat. When Athens, in 460, made an alliance with Argos, which was an enemy to Sparta, a state of war technically existed between the two great powers. And it went on for fourteen years, although the battles were fought for the most part on other people's land, with occasional raids by the Athenian fleet on Spartan ports and attacks by Pericles in and around the gulf of Corinth. In the winter of 446, the Spartan king signed a thirty years' peace between Sparta and Athens, but the following year he was sent into exile and the Spartans believed he had been bribed by Pericles. It was only a matter of time before hostilities started again.

When the second Peloponnesian war began in 431, the Greek world was split in two. It lasted for twenty-seven years and there was fighting for most of that time in most parts of Greece.

Thucydides

In following the story of the second Peloponnesian War, we meet our second historian, a man who made a most careful record of what happened. In contrast with Herodotus, whose lively narratives had inspired him to write history, Thucydides was aware of the need to be meticulous in selecting and verifying his sources. He is critical of Herodotus for writing as a public performer and entertainer rather than a careful seeker after the truth. Herodotus was writing to be heard, whereas Thucydides was, possibly for the first time, writing to be read. But he was keen to make it clear that he wasn't striving to be enjoyable:

It may well be that my history will seem less easy to read because of the absence in it of a romantic element. It will be enough for me, however, if these words of mine are judged useful by those who want to understand clearly the events which happened in the past and which (human nature being what it is) will, at some time or other and in much the same ways, be repeated in the future. My work was not a piece of writing designed to meet the taste of an immediate public, but was done to last forever. [THUCYDIDES 1972; P 48]

Thucydides is the historian's historian. He was highly intelligent. In fact, his work has been described as 'the product of a powerful brain, probably the most powerful that has ever addressed itself to historical writing' [Grant 1989; p 158]. He believed that history is good for you because human minds don't change any more than human bodies do, which means that humans will be constantly getting themselves into the same sort of mess and can learn how to get out of it if they know how it was done last time. So he was more interested in accuracy than readability. His style was described by the first Professor of Rhetoric at Rome, Quintilian, who prided himself on knowing good from bad writing, as '*densus et brevis et semper instans tibi*', delightfully translated by Ross Leckie as 'constipated and indigestible and always standing on its own toes' [Leckie 1989; p 47]. It has, for schoolmasters, the supreme merit of being difficult and this is no doubt why Thucydides was chosen by Thomas Arnold as an author to be studied in the reformed public schools of the mid-nineteenth century. Don't worry: we shall tackle him only in translation.

Thucydides makes us spectators of great events and sits us down close to them by quoting at great length the speeches which were made. This may seem oddly imaginative in a writer who claims to have avoided the romantic element, since clearly the speeches are, for the most part, made up. They are, in fact the parts of Thucydides where he is at his most constipated and obscure. He took the trouble to explain how he set about writing them:

I have found it difficult to remember the precise words used in the speeches which I listened to myself and my various informants have experienced the same difficulty; so my method has been, while keeping as close as possible to the general sense of the words that were actually used, to make the speakers say what, in my opinion, was called for by each situation.   [THUCYDIDES 1972; p 47]

We do not have the time or space to follow Thucydides through the Peloponnesian Wars, but we can get a flavour of his style from one famous incident. The small island of Melos in the Cyclades has become famous from the discovery there, in the early nineteenth century, of the Venus de Milo. In 416, more than two centuries before she was created, the islanders were trying to live a peaceful and uninvolved life, neither siding with Sparta, from which they originated, nor with Athens, who pressed them to join the alliance. So the Athenians sent an expedition there to persuade them. Thucydides tells us there were thirty Athenian ships, six from Chios, and two from Lesbos; 1200 hoplites (infantry), 300 archers and twenty mounted archers, all from Athens; and about 1200 hoplites from the allies and the surrounding islanders. The Athenians camped on Melos and, before doing any harm to the Melians, sent representatives to explain to the people why they were there.

The Melians refused to allow them to speak before the general assembly of the people, but a debate was held with a small number, forming the governing body, and Thucydides reports it in full.

They first agreed the rules for the debate and then the Athenians opened by saying that they would not waste time with fine phrases about rights and justice:

... *since you know as well as we do that when these matters are discussed by practical people, the standard of justice depends on the power to compel and that in fact the strong do what they have the power to do and the weak accept what they have to accept.*

Melians: Then in our view (since you force us to leave justice out of account and to confine ourselves to self-interest) — in our view it is at any rate useful that you should not destroy a principle that is to the general good of all men — namely that, in the case of all who fall into danger, there should be such a thing as fair play and just dealing, and that such people should be allowed to use and to profit by arguments that fall short of mathematical accuracy. [THUCYDIDES 1972; P402]

They go on to point out that the Athenians should, even though they are powerful, set an example of fairness because if they should fall from power, the most terrible vengeance could be taken on them. The Athenians reply to this that they are not at all concerned about future possibilities but only the present reality which is that the Melians must submit for their own and the Athenians' good. The debate continues:

Melians: And how can it be just as good for us to be slaves as for you to be the masters?

Athenians: You, by giving in, would save yourselves from disaster; we, by not destroying you, would be able to profit from you.

Melians: So you would not agree to our being neutral, friends instead of enemies, but allies of neither side?

Athenians: No, because it is not so much your hostility that injures us; it is rather the case that, if we were on friendly terms with you, our subjects would regard that as a sign of weakness in us, whereas your hatred is evidence of our power.   [IBID; P 402]

For six pages of close argument the reasoning is pursued as notions of fair play, right and wrong, are set aside by the Athenians in the light of Realpolitik. There can be no friendship between Athens and neutral states because those who remain neutral think their neutrality is a sign of their strength and of the weakness of Athens. The Melians try to meet the Athenians on their own ground by suggesting that the Spartans might come to their aid, but the Athenians point out that they are again looking to the future and should think of the present. They are offered an alliance on a tribute-paying basis with liberty to enjoy their lives and property: 'This is a safe rule – to stand up to one's equals, to behave with deference to one's superiors, and to treat one's inferiors with moderation.'

The Athenians then leave the discussion to allow the Melians to come to a decision after the long debate. When they return, the reply is ready:

Melians: Our decision, Athenians, is just the same as it was at first. We are not prepared to give up in a short moment the liberty which our city has enjoyed from its foundation for 700 years. We put our trust in the fortune that the gods will send and which has saved us up to now, and in the help of men – that is of the Spartans; and so we shall try to save ourselves. But we invite you to allow us to be friends of yours and enemies to neither side, to make a treaty which shall be agreeable to both you and us, and so to leave our country.   [IBID; P 407]

But the Athenians did not weaken: they continued their siege of the island and, when the Melians eventually surrendered, they killed all the men of military age and sold the women and children as slaves.

The Peloponnesian War was recorded in minute detail by Thucydides and you can follow its progress in his pages. It was a messy and disorganized conflict of battles interrupted by periods of what Thucydides calls a 'festering peace'. The Athenians made a couple of catastrophic miscalculations which finally caused their defeat. They supported two rebellious Persian satraps against the Persian king, which gave Persia a reason to support Sparta and they sent a fleet against Sicily in 415, which was routed at Syracuse in 413. Even then Athens fought on until Sparta, with the help of Persian money, forced her to capitulate after the battle of Aegospotami and a subsequent blockade of the Hellespont.

At this time we could have had a repetition of the scene on Melos: the Spartan army could have enslaved or killed the Athenians and burned the city to the ground. By the Athenians' own arguments, such a course of action would have been perfectly reasonable: 'the strong do what they have the power to do'. The city was spared because of what she had meant to Greeks and because even the Spartans recognized that Athens had become the brightest ornament of the civilized world.

Notable Dates

c. **2000**	First Cretan palaces built
15th century	Minoan civilization supreme
1400	Knossos destroyed
14th & 13th cent.	Mycenean civilization supreme
1230–1225	Fall of Troy
12th cent.	Destruction of Mycenae
c. **1000**	Dorian invasion
9th cent.	Foundation of Sparta
800	Appearance of the polis
776	First Olympic Games
	Homer: *Iliad*
8th cent.	Homer: *Odyssey*
7th cent.	Hesiod
621	Draco's laws
594	Solon's reforms
561–528	Peisistratos tyrant at Athens
512	Darius of Persia conquers Thrace
508–507	Cleisthenes' reforms at Athens
499	Revolt of Ionia against Persia
490	First Persian invasion. Battle of Marathon
483	Discovery of new vein of silver at Laurium
480	Second Persian invasion. Battles of Thermopylae and Salamis
479	Battles of Plataea and Mycale. Persians retreat from Greece
477	Delian League founded
461–446	First Peloponnesian War
460	Pericles takes charge in Athens
454	Treasury of Delian League transferred to Athens
447	Parthenon begun
446	Thirty Years' Peace between Athens and Sparta
445–431	Age of Pericles
431–404	Second Peloponnesian War
429	Death of Pericles
404	Athens surrenders to Sparta

CHAPTER TWO

Biology and the Life Sciences

The Greeks would never have thought of giving the name 'biology' to the science as we know it. *Bios* in Greek means life, not as opposed to death but as a way of living or course of life, usually applied to humans. The *biologos* or biologist existed, but seems to have been a sort of performer or mime artist, not a scientist. The German naturalist Gottfried Reinhold first used the word *Biologie* in its present sense as the title of a book published in 1802, and the name, for some reason, stuck.

When we read the beautiful Greek myth of how the moon fell in love with Endymion as he lay sleeping in a cave and visited him there nightly to sooth him asleep with gentle kisses so that he lay there for centuries in eternal youth and beauty, it's hard to imagine that the Greeks could teach us anything about science – when we have brought chunks of the moon back to earth to examine under electronic microscopes and know it's a piece of dead rock precisely 4600 million years old.

But we have a tendency to underestimate the common sense of those who lived in what we loftily call a 'pre-scientific' age. The stock argument goes, you remember, something like this: primitive man, in awe of the great forces of nature over which he had no control, invested them with personalities and came to think of them as gods and goddesses to be appeased and placated with sacrifices so that earthquakes could be avoided and harvests would be plentiful. It appeals, of course, to the paternalism in all of us to think of the Greeks as simple trusting people whose world was inhabited by controlling gods, goddesses and nature spirits, sowing their seed in season with a prayer to Demeter and watching, with the humble gratitude born of ignorance, the annual miracle of the sprouting crop.

But Greek peasants knew full well that if they didn't plant the seed there would be no crop and that if they planted it out of season or in the wrong soil, or there wasn't enough rain, no amount of prayer to Demeter would prevent it from withering. In other words, we tend to exaggerate the irrational naivety of those who lived before us.

Of course the Greeks believed in the interference of the gods in their world. Their geography and climate taught them as much. You don't have to live for long on an island in the Aegean today to realize that you are not in control; every summer is either unprecedentedly hot and dry or cold and wet; planes are suddenly grounded by unexpected squalls; even the huge ferry boats have to run for cover when a storm whips up the sea into ten-metre waves. Secure in a northern European town or city, we find the weather is irrelevant and something to take an interest in only at weekends. Here on a Greek island, even today, it affects what you get to eat, whether the post arrives and whether you can manage to go anywhere. So daily experience tells you that forces over which you have no control and only limited knowledge are directly influencing your life.

Because prayers were not always answered and sacrifices often failed to bring about the solution to these problems, the Greeks thought of their gods as moody and unpredictable – a not unreasonable inference to draw from the observable evidence. And at quite an early date they became sceptical about the ancient myths. The sceptics had a spokesman in Xenophanes of Colophon, an Ionian who lived somewhere between 570–470 and had the nerve to attack Homer and Hesiod, the twin pillars of Greek education, for their teachings about the gods: 'Homer and Hesiod have attributed to the gods everything that amongst men earns shame and abuse – theft, adultery and mutual deceit.' He even went on to develop an impious thought:

If oxen and lions and horses had hands like men and could draw and make works of art, horses would make gods look like horses, and oxen like oxen, and each would draw pictures of the gods as if they had bodies like their own.   [QUOTED JACT 1984; P 282]

It follows that the gods, who are described as having the appetites and the physical appearance of men, must be the creations of men: 'Ethiopians have black, snub-nosed gods, and Thracians have blue-eyed, red-haired gods.' Having discredited the Olympians as the controlling power that influence natural phenomena, Xenophanes left the field open for objective scientific observation.

Ionia

Greek science, which was not, in the early stages, thought of as different from Greek philosophy, began, not on the Greek mainland nor even in the Greek islands, but on the coast of Asia Minor, among the cities of Ionia. These had been settled by the end of the tenth century by immigrants from mainland Greece with the encouragement of the Athenians who had even then a powerful navy. The Ionians prospered, having 'a better climate than any other we know of' [Herodotus 1, 142], a fertile soil, and a rich trade with the Greek islands and with Egypt, from where they bought perfumes, ivory and ebony. Miletus, the most important city, founded a chain of successful colonies on the shores of the Black Sea, and had a considerable trade with Sybaris in Southern Italy, while Phocaea had set up a colony as far west as Marseilles.

Ionia has a reputation for being the birthplace of free thinking in Greece, where the traditional patterns of thought about religion and myths were first questioned. These attitudes are typified in a poem by the seventh-century poet Archilochus. The story was well known and much admired of the Spartan mother who said to her son as he left for battle, 'Come back with your shield or on it'. To lose the shield was the ultimate disgrace and it would be better that her son's body be carried home on the shield than that he should humiliate his family by losing it in battle. Archilochus takes a different view:

Some lucky Thracian has my noble shield;
I had to run; I dropped it in a wood.
But I got clear away thank God! So hang
The shield! I'll get another just as good.   [QUOTED KITTO 1951; P 88]

The importance of this changed attitude is that it rejected the unthinking acceptance of tradition as a guide to life. Only when people refuse to accept the principle that it is best to do things as they have always been done does it become possible to ask the questions and seek for the answers that are at the foundation of science. The Ionians took this step.

The field of Greek science, like all areas of investigation widely ranged over by scholars, is beset with traps and snares. There is a central debate which those of us on the outer reaches can be aware of, that is between the 'instrumentalists' and the 'realists'. The instrumentalists hold that a scientific theory should yield predictions that correspond to the observed data and therefore need be no more than calculating devices in relation to them; the realists say that a scientific theory must be more than that: it must be also true of the underlying realities.

The first of the scientist/philosophers of Ionia was Thales of Miletus, born about 624, who is famous in Histories of Philosophy for predicting a solar eclipse which took place on 28 May 585. He did this, it is claimed, by using a cycle of eclipses familiar to the Babylonians which he learned about during his travels in Egypt. Histories of Astronomy tend to be sceptical about this, pointing out that the Babylonians knew of no such cycle and that the best he might have done was to forecast the likelihood of an eclipse within a year or so. It's tempting to come to the conclusion that the astronomers think of Thales as a great philosopher while the philosophers think of him as a great astronomer. What he really did is not easy to establish because none of his writings has survived. But Aristotle thought highly of him, quoted some of his doctrines, and said he was the first real philosopher. Philosophy, by the way, didn't mean at the time 'love of knowledge', as we're told today; it probably meant a devotion to uncommon knowledge, or love of the quirky.

Thales at least behaved like a scientist; there's a famous story of his gazing at the stars and falling into a well rather in the style of the modern professor who boiled his watch while gazing at the egg. But

Thales showed that brains have their uses; his meteorological studies brought to his notice one year certain signs which told him that the next crop of olives would be a large one. So he quietly bought an option on all the olive presses in the district so that when the large harvest came and everybody wanted to press out the oil at the same time, he was able to make a killing on hire charges.

He also dabbled in useful activities: as an astronomer, he was able to point out to the Milesian sailors the constellation of the Little Bear, which revolves around the North Pole in a smaller circle than the Great Bear and is more useful for navigation; as a mathematician, he worked out that the height of a building is related to the length of its shadow exactly as the height of any vertical object is related to its shadow at the same time of day. He is said to have picked this up in Egypt and used it to measure the pyramids. He is also credited with having worked out and proved that a circle is bisected by its diameter, that the angles at the base of an isosceles triangle are equal and that vertically opposed angles are equal.

But Thales was most famous for asking what must have seemed the most useless question of all time, and yet it's one on which we're currently spending billions of dollars a year in researching; what is everything made of? The particle accelerator at the Fermilab High Energy Physics Research Centre near Chicago was set up to answer this question, and so is the super conductivity collider planned for Waxahachie, just south of Dallas, Texas, which will be 84 kilometres (52 miles) in diameter and cost around twelve million dollars. It will be operated by a team of highly trained, highly skilled and highly paid scientists to probe into what Thales puzzled about sitting on a rock on the coast of Asia Minor two and a half thousand years ago.

Thales managed to find an answer: water. We shall never know how he worked it out, though he had travelled in Egypt and seen the annual miracle of the dead land being brought to life by the flood waters of the Nile. Egyptian and Babylonian myths suggest that the earth rests on water. Thales could see that water fell from the skies, surrounded the dry land and gushed out of the earth. It was in the split tree and under the lifted stone. It could exist as solid, liquid, or gas. But the most interesting thing is not the answer, but the question. It served no practical purpose, unlike the forecast of the olive harvest. The pragmatic Romans would never have thought of asking it. And the assumption behind it is fundamental to the way the Greeks thought. Behind all the complexities of life, material and moral, there must be simple principles. All the many manifestations of matter must come from one basic stuff just as the apparent complexities in the moral universe must hide simple knowable principles. It was a basic faith, rather like that of Einstein: 'God may be subtle, but he is not malicious,' he said, accepting that God wouldn't make the universe more complicated than he had to. There has to be a basic, predictable formula: 'God does not play at dice.' That was the way things looked from the Institute for Advanced Study of Princeton University and so they appeared on the coast of Asia Minor in 600 BC: apparent differences must hide a real unity. The universe is an ordered structure, a cosmos, as contrasted with the chaos or formless void which existed before things were made to shape up. So there is a point in looking for basic laws in Nature because the world is rationally organized. It is a principle we shall come across throughout Greek thought.

Anaximander, a younger contemporary of Thales, born about 610, who was his pupil and possibly a relative, also lived at Miletus and wore splendid clothes. Thales has been called the first Greek philosopher because he abandoned traditional myths as explanations of reality. Anaximander may well have launched scientific method if we accept Karl Popper's claim that this consists in the challenging of falsifiable theses because he challenged his master's thesis about the basic substance. He said simply that the changes we see around us, the birth and death, growth and decay, are the result of the conflict between opposites: hot and cold, wet and dry etc. Since water, being wet, was one of these pairs of opposites, it could not be the primal stuff. Quite what he decided was the primal element is not entirely clear. He called it to *apeiron*, the Indefinite and described it as 'eternal and ageless':

It is neither water nor any other of the so-called elements, but a nature different from them and infinite from which arise all the heavens and worlds within them.

[QUOTED KIRK & RAVEN 1957; P 106]

We need not follow Anaximander and his critics into the metaphysics of his Indefinite, which belong more to philosophy than to science, but we can note that he also applied himself to more useful pursuits: he was the first to draw a map of the inhabited world as it was then known for the Milesian sailors on the Black Sea; he also introduced the gnomon, a vertical rod which indicates the sun's direction and height, and is said to have set up the first sundial at Sparta. He was the first to attempt to give a rational explanation for the origin of mankind in which he anticipated modern ideas by claiming that all life comes from the sea and that the animals around us have evolved from primitive forms by adaptation to their environment. He even worked out that man must have descended from animals of another species because 'while other animals quickly find nourishment for themselves, man alone needs a lengthy period of suckling, so that, had he been originally as he is now, he could never have survived'.

Anaximenes was the third member of what is now called the Milesian School of philosophers because of their connections with the Ionian town of Miletus. He also had a go at the basic problem of what everything is made of and came up with air. It's not hard to see how he might have felt that air is the principle of all life, since we have to breathe it to live and the breath or wind or air had long been identified with the soul; but he had something of a struggle to explain how solid objects and all matter might be made up of air. He did this by ingeniously suggesting the effects of compressing or rarefying air. He pointed out that if we blow air in a stream from our mouths it is compressed and therefore cool, whereas if we open our mouths and allow air to drift out without compression, it is warm. So compressed air could become wind, clouds, water, earth and eventually stones, whereas rarefied air heated up and became fire. How many people believed him has not been recorded.

Pythagoras, the first of the early philosopher scientists to have a name that still resonates in our minds today, was born about 560 on the island of Samos, close to Miletus. He travelled widely in Egypt and claimed to have learned much from the priests of Heliopolis, Memphis and Thebes. He returned to become tutor to the tyrant of Samos but they didn't get on and Pythagoras set off for Italy, settling at Croton, on the south coast, just under the ball of the big toe. He had by this time acquired a number of followers and they formed themselves into a religious community, set apart from the rest of society and united in living by a series of bizarre rules:

1. Not to eat beans.
2. Not to walk in the main street.
3. Not to stir the fire with iron.
4. Not to touch a white cock.
5. Not to eat the heart.
6. Not to stand upon the parings of their nails.
7. Not to leave the impression of the body on the bed when getting up.
8. To efface the traces of a pot in the ashes.
9. To help a man who is loading freight but not one who is unloading.
10. Not to look in a mirror beside a lamp.

[IAMBLICHUS, *Protrepticus*, 21, QUOTED KIRK & RAVEN 1957; PP 226-7]

The prohibition against beans has aroused much interest among scholars. Some have suggested that the beans were voting counters and that what is prohibited is some form of democracy; others hold that Pythagoras may have suffered from an allergy and wanted to protect his followers; Aristotle thought he might have taken against beans because they are shaped like testicles. But the most delightful though least likely explanation is that eating beans causes breaking wind; wind is soul; so eating beans causes the dissipation of the soul.

The soul was certainly given a new importance by Pythagoras, or by Pythagoreans. We are unsure which, because Pythagoras is another famous man of this time who left no writings at all. He was even cagey about passing on his teachings, giving instruction only to a closed circle of initiates who were bound by a rule of secrecy. Many of the ideas attributed to him were no doubt thought up by later followers who then attached his name to give them authority. We shall never know what Pythagoras discovered; but we do have records of what Pythagoreans taught.

The basis of their religious belief was in the transmigration of souls. There is a story recorded in the life of Pythagoras by Diogenes Laertius, that the philosopher once called out to somebody to stop beating a dog because he could recognize, in the dog's yelping, the voice of a friend. Since we can't be sure in what life forms our dead friends may turn up, it isn't safe to eat any of them and it's a bad idea to have anything to do with butchers and huntsmen. But vegetarianism is not the most important consequence of the doctrine of metempsychosis. Since what we might be born into in the next life depends on our behaviour in this one, there is a strong motivation to right conduct. The followers of Pythagoras all hoped, by sticking to the rules, to be born again as nobility; if they broke any, they might expect to turn up as a woman, a pig, a dog, or even a tree.

In this, their most famous teaching, the Pythagoreans were drawing heavily on the Eastern religions, but they influenced the Greek philosophers by reawakening an interest in the soul. Most of the Milesians seem to have been materialists, or at least were not preoccupied with spiritual matters, and the literary inheritance from Homer had pictured human souls as gibbering shades who longed to be back in the world. For the Pythagoreans, the soul was immortal, hence the most important part of the person, and its well-being the proper focus of living. These ideas were to be picked up and developed by Socrates and Plato.

One of the myths of Dionysus used to justify the teachings of the Pythagoreans told how the god had been eaten by the Titans who were then blasted by the fire of Zeus. From their ashes, Zeus then created a new race of men whose natures were formed from the eaters and the eaten. So all men have a lot of carnality and a little divinity within them. The mortal body (soma) is the tomb (sema) in which the spirit is buried.

By perceiving the truth in Nature, the Pythagoreans taught, a man can purify himself and gradually eradicate the Titanic elements that are within him. And this truth in Nature was, for them, the form, order, proportion and harmony which have been imposed on chaos, and which form mathematical truths. So the purification of the soul can be achieved through the study of mathematics, which brings us to the contribution of Pythagoreans to early Greek science.

We remember Pythagoras today mainly because of his infamous theorem which crops up in every school maths exam; that the square on the hypotenuse of a right-angled triangle is equal to the sum of the squares on the other two sides. The Egyptians knew it and used it in the construction of the pyramids; the Babylonians had worked out that the numbers could be 3, 4 and 5 or even 6, 8 and 10 or any combination where the largest number squared is equal to the sum of the squares of the other two numbers; but Pythagoras is said to have been the first to work out a geometrical proof. He was so pleased with himself when he finally managed it that he sacrificed a hundred oxen in celebration and possibly gratitude.

His delight in numbers was not only because the study of them led to purification of the soul. Numbers and their relationships had, for the Pythagoreans, a mystical, absolute, even divine status in themselves. An indication of this, they claimed, is that the pitch of a lyre string is proportionate to its length and that there is a direct relationship between the notes of a musical scale and numerical ratios. If a string is halved in length, it sounds an octave above; a ratio in lengths of 2 to 3 gives the musical interval of a fifth. So a string 12 units long gives a base note, of which a string 8 units long sounds a fifth above and one 6 units long an octave above. As the octave and the fifth sound harmonious, there is a 'harmonic progression' between the numbers 6, 8 and 12. A cube has what the Pythagoreans would call a 'geometrical harmony' because it has 6 sides, 8 corners and 12 edges.

Because counting was often done with pebbles, they were able to show the satisfying relationships between 'figurate numbers', that is, the ones made by counting in patterns. So, using triangular shapes we have 1 ., 3 .., 6 ∴ and 10 ⸪. The last is the perfect number, since it is made up of $1 + 2 + 3 + 4 = 10$. Because the number 10, if made up as a triangular shape constructed out of pebbles or dots, has four on each side, it was known as *tetractys*, was thought to be holy, and the Pythagoreans swore by it.

They were also concerned with 'perfect numbers', being the ones which are a sum of their factors added together. So 6 is perfect, being $1 + 2 + 3$, and so is 28, being $1 + 2 + 4 + 7 + 14$. The next is 496, then 8128 and then there's nothing till 2 096 128, which must have taken some time to work out. But the Pythagoreans working on it were purifying their souls and had few distractions. One of them might have been the search for 'amicable numbers', that is two numbers one of which is equal to the sum of the factors of the other; the factors of 220 are 1,2,4,5,10,11,20,22,44,55 and 110. If you add these up you get 284. So 220 and 284 are amicable numbers. They are the only ones to have been known in antiquity and they were discovered, so the tradition goes, by Pythagoras himself.

Some of us find the study of numbers, whether figurate, perfect or amicable, rather hard going, while to others it can be an amusing intellectual game. But to the Pythagoreans, numbers were the stable reality at the heart of the Universe in which they saw change and decay. So numbers had a mystic eternal quality. It's a belief that can still be found amongst the pure mathematicians of our own time.

Tradition has it that Pythagoras was the first philosopher to call himself one. His followers, set apart in their closed community, heard the Master speak to them each evening from behind a curtain. Few of them were allowed to see him. Those who did so reported that the experience enriched the rest of their lives and that he had long flowing locks, a white robe and, as a special mark of distinction, a golden thigh.

The Pythagoreans had split by the end of the fifth century into a scientific group who followed his investigations into music, astronomy, arithmetic and geometry and a religious group who tried to purify themselves by going barefoot and abstaining from meat and beans. The descendants of both groups can still be seen around us today.

Medicine

The earliest records of Greek medicine are in Homer, who tells us that the first doctor was Asclepius, son of Apollo and Father of Medicine. He learned medicine from his father – Apollo was, among other things, the god of healing as well as of sickness – and became so skilled that he could even raise people from the dead. When Zeus once heard that he had done this for gold, he struck down both Asclepius and his patient with a thunderbolt, but later restored Asclepius to life. His image, holding the curative serpent, was set among the stars. The snake was an image of restoration because each year it sloughs its skin.

The sons of Asclepius, Podaleirius and Machaon, were the physicians who attended the Greek army at the siege of Troy. Podaleirus was a physician who healed wounds by using herbs and was the first to diagnose the madness of Ajax from his flashing eyes; Machaon was equally skilled but as a surgeon who could cut out arrow heads and trim back the decaying flesh from old wounds. He was killed at Troy.

Sickness of any kind was, like any other human predicament for which there is no obvious explanation, put down to the visitation of the gods and healing was widely credited to Asclepius who had temples all over Greece. The most famous, at Epidaurus, had a sanctuary where priests would hand out cures ranging from charms to snake bites in return for votive offerings. Many of those who offered gifts and prayers to Asclepius were healed and his cult spread over Greece, one of the sacred snakes being taken from Epidaurus to Athens to authenticate a shrine there. It stayed for a time with Sophocles. The reputation of Asclepius was widespread and secure since his priests did nothing to interfere with the natural healing processes and, although there is a great deal of difference between a good doctor and a bad doctor, there is very little difference between a good doctor and no doctor at all.

Hippocrates

But then came the real Father of Medicine, one of the Greeks whose name is still with us and whose ideals affect our lives today through the influence of his famous Oath: Hippocrates. He attacked the superstition of the cult magicians and spent his life promoting the pursuit of medicine through careful observation and rational deduction. His most famous passage is on the 'sacred' disease, epilepsy:

> The facts about the so-called 'sacred' disease are as follows. I don't think it is any more sacred and divine than any other disease, it has its own symptoms and cause, but because of men's inexperience and its extraordinary character men supposed it had a divine origin. I think that the kind of men who first attributed a sacred quality to this disease were similar to today's magicians, Salvationists, quacks and charlatans who all claim to be very religious and to have superior knowledge. Because they felt helpless and had no effective treatment to suggest, they took refuge in the pretence of divinity and treated the disease as sacred to conceal their own ignorance.   [QUOTED JACT 1984; p101]

Hippocrates has come down to us as one of the great scientific humanists of the past and it comes as a bit of a shock to find that modern scholars have as yet been unable to upset the judgement of the distinguished German classicist Wilamowitz that he is no more than *ein berühmter Name ohne den Hintergrund irgend einer Schrift*, which sonorous comment means, 'a famous name without the background of even a single piece of writing'. All of the texts which were once thought to have come from his hand have been challenged and, although we can visit his birthplace today on the island of Kos and be shown the ruins of the temple where he taught, it seems that we can no longer be absolutely sure of anything he is supposed to have said because none of the treatises which bear his name can be safely attributed to him.

But that Hippocrates existed, and was known as a great doctor who charged fees for his services is testified by both Plato and Aristotle, and the medical practices that bear his name are recorded in treatises of the fifth and fourth centuries. One of the most famous, *On the Sacred Disease*, quoted above, is clearly written, not only to reveal the truth about a disease, but to attack an opposing method of treatment. And the many texts, grouped under a general name of 'Hippocratic', have been so classified, not because they can safely be traced back to an author, but because they seem to preach the same methods.

In classical Greece there were no recognised medical academies; doctors could not put up a plate at their doors decorated with the initials M.D. Every type of treatment was opposed to every other in a Thatcherian marketplace where success brought money and failure destitution. And in the true spirit of naked capitalism, success depended on the failure of competitors. So the true physician, if he wanted to be successful, had to devote part of his energies to discrediting the opposition, and this is clearly what many of the Hippocratic texts sought to do. There were many traditionalists in the field, ranging from the resident temple priests to the itinerant charlatans selling charms. These all preached that illness had a supernatural cause and so could only be cured by invoking supernatural aid.

The Hippocratics opposed this. They taught that diseases were part of nature and had natural causes. Their methods of treatment were founded on the careful observation and recording of the symptoms and progress of diseases so that a body of case histories became available to the doctor on which he could base a reasonable prognosis. As for treatment, the stress is on diet and rest, the knowledge that time is a great healer, and a good bedside manner. It is a good idea to make up your mind, before entering the sick room, what you intend to do, based on your knowledge of case histories; this makes a good impression and is pretty easy:

When you do go in, be careful how you sit and maintain your reserve. Be careful of your dress, be authoritative in what you say, but be brief, be reassuring and sympathetic, show care and reply to objections, meet any difficulties with calm assurance, forbid noise and disturbance, be ready to do what has to be done.

[HIPPOCRATES *Decorum* 7-13, QUOTED JACT 1984; P 191.]

It would be difficult for our BMA public relations experts today to come up with anything better. But the Hippocratic doctors were concerned with more than appearances; the oath bound them to a standard of medical ethics which has survived into our own time:

I will follow that system of regimen which, according to my ability and judgment I consider for the benefit of my patients, and abstain from whatever is deleterious and mischievous. I will give no deadly medicine to anyone, if asked, nor suggest any such counsel; and in like manner I will not give to any woman a pessary to procure abortion. With purity and with holiness I will pass my life and practise my Art. I will not cut persons labouring under the stone, but will leave this to be done by men who are practitioners of this work. Into whatever houses I enter, I will go into them for the benefit of the sick, and will abstain from every voluntary act of mischief and corruption; and further, from the seduction of females and males, of freemen and slaves. Whatever, in connection with my professional practice or not, in connection with it, I see or hear, in the life of men, which ought not to be spoke of abroad, I will not divulge, as reckoning that all such should be kept secret. While I continue to keep this Oath unviolated, may it be granted to me to enjoy life and the practice of the art respected by all men in all times. But should I trespass and violate this Oath may the reverse be my lot.   [HIPPOCRATES 1939; P 18]

It is not easy to assess just how effective Hippocratic medicine was because many of the herbal remedies cannot be identified. Of the more common ones, garlic still holds its place as a therapeutic plant, though from some of the places in which it was inserted, its virtues might well not have found their way very easily around the body. Cabbage water was popular, being readily available; at the other end of the dietary spectrum were the substances which drew their miraculous authority from the difficulty of obtaining them, such as the liver of a turtle ground up with the milk of a mother who was suckling a male child.

Another difficulty in assessing the effectiveness of the remedies is that the dosage is rarely specified. And this is the result of an insight into the nature of illness frequently overlooked today, namely that patients differ; that although diseases may be the same, they affect people differently and so the cures, both in their nature and their quantities, have to be individually tailored. As part of their consideration of the patient as a whole, the Hippocratics were careful to study his diet and to prescribe changes where these seemed necessary. Because older people seem to dry out somewhat, the Hippocratic doctors believed that they should drink more liquids. They based their treatment on observation and the keeping of records which gave rise to a series of aphorisms, many of which are accepted wisdom today. Here is a selection of them. The first is the best-known, though we don't normally associate it with medical wisdom, since the Romans turned it into a proverb:

Life is short and the Art long; the occasion fleeting; experience fallacious, and judgment difficult. The physician must not only be prepared to do what is right himself, but also to make the patient, the attendants and externals cooperate.

When in a state of hunger, one ought not to undertake labour.

Drinking strong wine cures hunger.

It is better that a fever succeed to a convulsion than a convulsion succeed to a fever.

Purgative medicines agree ill with persons in good health.

An article of food or drink which is slightly worse, but more palatable, is to be preferred to such as are better but less palatable.

Of two pains occurring together, not in the same part of the body, the stronger weakens the other.

Largeness of person is noble in youth and not unbecoming; but in old age it is inconvenient and worse than a smaller structure.

Sneezing coming on, in the case of a person with a hiccup, removes the hiccup.

A few of the aphorisms seem unlikely, such as the claim that maniacs who develop piles become sane, or:

Eunuchs do not take the gout, nor become bald.

A woman does not take the gout unless her menses be stopped.

A young man does not take the gout until he indulges in coition.

If a woman do not conceive, and wishes to ascertain whether she can conceive, having wrapped her up in blankets, fumigate below, and if it appear that the scent passes through the body to the nostrils and mouth, know that of herself she is not unfruitful.

[HIPPOCRATES 1939; PP 299-329]

They had an attitude to pain different from ours; the word *ponos* which means a sustained pain is also the word used for toil or labour. And, just as labour is natural and necessary to agriculture, so pain is part of the healing process. When the pain became excessive, the Hippocratic doctors prescribed opium.

There was a general belief amongst them that the human body was made up of four basic constituents and that the fundamental cause of illness was an imbalance between these constituents. There are differences of detail, but the general view was that these constituents were blood, which is hot, phlegm which is cold, yellow bile which is dry and black bile which is wet. These again were associated with the basic natural elements, fire, earth, air, and water. Within the corpus of Hippocratic writings there are several incompatible theories as to what these basic constituents are, but the notion that illness proceeds from an imbalance of basic elements is common.

There have been enthusiasts for the Hippocratic school who have claimed that it laid the foundations of modern scientific medicine and there have been – such is the contentious nature of scholarship – those who have denied that the Hippocratic doctors were in any real sense scientific, since they based their work on a fundamental misconception of human physiology. They may, it is said, have established method in medicine; but method is only effective if you know how the body actually works.

What does seem fair to claim for them is that they were the first doctors to explain human illness by purely natural, and not supernatural, causes; that they first realized the importance of careful observation and recording of the progress of disease; that they first stressed that illnesses affect individuals differently and so treatment must be geared to individual patients; and that they first realized the importance of diet as an aid to healing. They were also the first professional doctors to recognize the healing power of nature; that organisms have the tendency, when damaged, to repair themselves and that the best doctors are those who assist and don't interfere with the process. And they did all of this in the open; they had no secret clubs, no exclusion of non-members. Hippocratic medicine was open for all to see, to criticize, and to participate in.

What exactly they understood by the 'whole' in approaching illness is not understood. Either it was the whole person, as a psychological and physiological unity, in which case they are well in line with current medical practice, or it was the person as an integral part of the natural world, whose setting in a wider sense – the seasons of the year, the winds, the location of the home – should be studied. If the second interpretation is right, Hippocratic medicine is closer to us today than it was a generation ago, since we are often told, in these days of inner city violence, that character is shaped by environment and that 'a person is – where he is'. Hippocrates anticipated this and accounts for that sense of superiority which all Northerners feel when travelling South, whether York-shiremen on a visit to the Home Counties or Canadians vacationing in Florida:

where the land is fertile, soft, and well-watered ... and where the seasons are fine, there the men are fleshy, have ill-formed joints and are of a humid temperament; they are not disposed to endure labour and, for the most part are base in spirit; indolence and sluggishness are visible in them, and to the arts they are sluggish and dull and not clever or acute.

When the country is bare, not fenced and rugged, blasted by the winter and scorched by the sun, there you may see the men hardy, slender, with well-shaped joints, well braced and shaggy; sharp vigilance and industry accompany such a constitution; in morals and passions they are haughty and opinionative, inclining to the fierce rather than the mild; and you will find them acute and ingenious as regards the arts and excelling in military affairs. [HIPPOCRATES 1939; P42]

Zoology

Take 20 eggs and let them be incubated by hens. Each day, from the second to that of hatching, remove an egg, break it, and examine it. You will find that the nature of the bird can be likened to that of man. The membranes proceed from the umbilical cord, and all that I have said on the subject of the infant, you will find in the bird's egg, in which you will be surprised to find an umbilical cord. [IBID; P43]

This instruction for the first controlled biological experiment in history is included in the Hippocratic collection of writings, dating from about 380. What we call zoology was relevant to medicine, since man is indisputably an animal when he's sick, whatever his spiritual aspirations might be, and these medical men studied the diet and habits of animals as an aid to their art. The Greeks seem to have had an unusually keen eye for the animal kingdom since from the earliest times their vase paintings and mosaics show animals – and especially marine creatures – with an astonishingly accurate attention to detail. In fact the Greek word for painter – *zoographos* – means simply somebody who draws animals. The Hippocratics even attempted to classify animals by their habits in a work called *On Diet*, but for a really thorough, exhaustive, not to say exhausting approach to the subject, we have to turn to Aristotle.

Aristotle

Because for so many generations the work of Aristotle was looked on with awe by scientists as well as philosophers, it might be salutary to begin with a dissenting note – especially as it had been expressed by a Nobel prizewinner with a fine flair for altercation. Sir Peter Medawar, in a judgement on Aristotle written jointly with his wife, draws our attention to the opinion of the philosopher and essayist Goldsworthy Lowes Dickinson:

Aristotle was a 'man of science' in the modern sense. He was a careful collector and observer of an enormous range of facts ... much of his work is still regarded with respect by scientists who care to study it.

The Medawars comment:

These two sentences ... betray an almost majestic incomprehension of the character of science and of Aristotle's influence on science in the modern sense. A scientist is no more a collector and classifier of facts than a historian is a man who compiles and classifies a chronology of the dates of great battles, major discoveries, and so on.

They go on to record the weary exasperation with which the real scientists of the seventeenth century tried to throw off the yoke of Aristotle and then give their own opinion of the extant corpus:

> The biological works of Aristotle are a strange and generally speaking rather tiresome farrago of hearsay, imperfect observation, wishful thinking, and credulity amounting to downright gullibility ... Sometimes of course Aristotle is right; his writings were so voluminous he could hardly fail to be correct sometimes (irreverent thoughts of monkeys and typewriters steal into the mind). [MEDAWAR & MEDAWAR 1984; p28]

It is as well to be aware of modern reservations when coming across the rich and varied but, it must be admitted, lengthy biological writings of Aristotle. But we can take heart in the opinion of an earlier scientist with credentials not inferior to those of the Medawars. On the appearance, in 1882, of an English translation of *The Parts of Animals*, Charles Darwin wrote to the translator:

> From quotations which I had seen, I had a high notion of Aristotle's merits, but I had not the most remote notion what a wonderful man he was. Linnaeus and Cuvier have been my two gods, though in very different ways, but they were mere schoolboys to old Aristotle [QUOTED ARISTOTLE 1945; pvi]

It seems to me that the first great contribution Aristotle made to the development of observational science was to justify it, as an acceptable human activity, to his philosophical colleagues. We have already noticed the tendency of the earliest philosopher/scientists to become preoccupied with the Big Questions such as the origin of the universe and the basic stuff of which it might be made. The reassuring aspect of such speculations is that they are difficult to disprove and that they don't involve getting your hands dirty or your feet wet. Aristotle wrote a tactful appeal for would-be scientists to get out and look:

> Natural objects fall into two great classes, the immortal ones that are without beginning and imperishable and those that are subject to generation and decay. The former are worthy of honour and are divine, but are less within the reach of our observation, for all our speculations about them and our aspirations after knowledge of them can only in the rarest instance be confirmed by direct perception. But with regard to the plants and animals that perish, we are better off for coming to a knowledge of them, for we are inhabitants of the same earth. Anyone who is willing to take the necessary trouble can learn a great deal about all the species

1 *Top* Achilles, the central heroic figure of the *Iliad*, slaying Penthesilea,
queen of the Amazons, who came to the aid of the Trojans after the death of Hector;
on an amphora from Vulci.

◄◇►◄◇►

2 *Above* Odysseus, hero of the *Odyssey*, after years of wandering, returns home disguised
as a beggar to his wife Penelope; terracotta relief of the fifth century BC.

3 Bronze statue, c.470–450 BC. If his right hand held a thunderbolt, this is Zeus; if it was a trident, Poseidon.

◄ ‹› ‹› ►

4 *Opposite* The dramatic sanctuary site of Delphi, built on the slopes of Mt Parnassus, the home of the oracle of Apollo, the most important in classical Greece. Every two years the Pythian Games were held in Apollo's honour, named after the priestess – the Pythia – through whom the oracle spoke. The photograph shows the Tholos, a circular building in the sanctuary of Athena Pronaia.

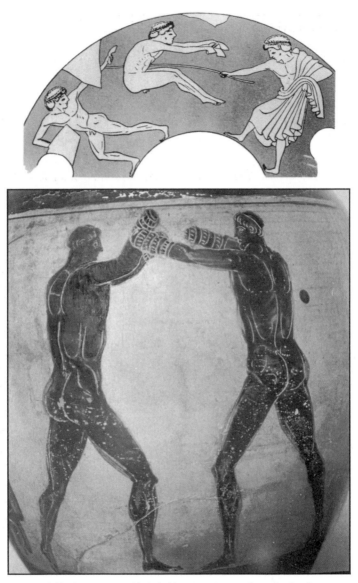

5 *Top* A jumper in mid-air holding jumping weights in his hands;
drawing based on an Athenian cup, c.490 BC.

⟨⟩⟨⟩⟨⟩

6 *Above* Two boxers, their hands bound with thongs, on an amphora
of the fourth century BC.

7 *Top* Two wrestlers practising their hold, with (left) a runner at the start, and (right) a spear-thrower testing his spear; marble relief from the base of a statue, late sixth century BC.

8 *Above* Athletes with javelin and discus, on a plate of the fourth century BC.

9 The bronze Charioteer, found in the sanctuary of Apollo at Delphi, a votive offering for victory in a chariot race; 470 BC.

◄◇►◄◇►

10 *Opposite* The 'Discus-Thrower', or Discobolos, a Roman marble copy of a bronze statue by the Athenian sculptor Myron, 460–450 BC.

11 The Calfbearer, marble statue found in the Athenian Acropolis, 575–550 BC.

12 *Left* Statue of a young girl, or *kore*, dressed in chiton and cloak, probably made on the island of Chios, 520–510 BC.

◄◄◄►►►

13 *Right* The youth Kroisos, made of marble from Paros, *c.*520 BC. The power of his body suggests a breaking away from the Archaic style.

14 Roman copy of Polyclitus' statue of Diadumenos, showing a youth binding
a fillet round his head, c.440–430 BC.

◄◄►◄►►

15 *Opposite* Bronze warrior, one of two found in 1972 in the sea near Riace
in southern Italy, c.450 BC.

16 *Above left* Marble statue of Hermes with the infant Dionysus in his arms,
by Praxiteles, 350–330 BC.

◄◄►◄►►

17 *Above right* Apoxyomenos, a Roman copy of a bronze original by Lysippus, c.325 BC.
The statue shows an athlete scraping his arms after bathing.

◄◄►◄►►

18 *Opposite* Athens: view of the Acropolis with Mount Lykabettus in the background,
seen from the Philopappus Hill.

19 *Top* An older man seducing a youth; from an Athenian amphora, c.540 BC.

⧯⧯⧯⧯⧯

20 *Above* Athenian youths with their girlfriends; from an Attic vase, c.500 BC.

⧯⧯⧯⧯⧯

21 *Opposite* Roman copy of the famous Aphrodite of Cnidos, c.340 BC. This statue, by Praxiteles, was widely held to be the greatest in antiquity; the original has never been found, but there are many Roman copies.

22 Bust of Socrates.

that exist. Both enquiries have their charm. Although in the case of the former we can achieve little owing to their being out of our reach, yet the veneration in which they are held imparts to knowledge of them a degree of pleasure greater than appertains to any of the things that are within our reach, as a lover would rather catch a random glimpse of his beloved than have a complete view of many other valuable things. But the latter, owing to our better and fuller acquaintance with them, have advantage from the scientific point of view. Indeed their nearness to us and their kinship with us may be said to counterbalance the claims of divine philosophy ... Let us then not shrink like children from the investigation of the humbler creatures. In every natural object there is something to excite our imagination.

[QUOTED FARRINGTON 1944; PP 157-8]

It must have been the excited imagination of Aristotle that kept him going through a vast pile of work. His biological writings were put together towards the end of his career, probably in the last twelve years of his life. They comprise the History of Animals, which, since the Greek word istoria means 'investigation' rather than 'history', should really be called Investigations into Animals, Parts of Animals, On the Generation of Animals, and On the Progressive Motion of Animals. These books are available in translation and, since they deal with birth, copulation and death, are close to all of us and a good read.

Of course there are the vulgar errors which irritate the Medawars: the idea that some birds, such as the partridge, and common fowls are particularly 'salacious' whilst the crows are inclined to chastity, or that some animals are good-tempered whilst others can be mean and treacherous. These set on edge the teeth of animal behaviourists today – though I would lay a heavy bet that their own explanations of the ways that animals conduct themselves will raise a few laughs a generation from now. Aristotle was able, from his own observations, to correct a few of the howlers current in his day. He was, for example, able to describe the joints in the legs of elephants and put an end to the belief that they had none and could only sleep by leaning against a tree.

It is the range and detail of his contributions to the study of the natural world which scientists have rightly found astonishing. The records put together by Aristotle contain details of the physical structure, the lives and the breeding habits of about 540 species of animals. Many of these involved dissection, such as the description of the eye of the mole or the stomach in ruminants. That Aristotle practised vivisection is clear from his comments on the movements of the heart of the tortoise after removal and of the trembling of the chameleon after dissection.

His observations of the octopus and squid have only been surpassed in modern times and some of his records, for example on the fact that the young of the dogfish is linked to the womb by a placental cord like a mammal, were doubted for many centuries before being confirmed. So impressed was the biologist Louis Agassiz by his discovery that Aristotle had been right after all about paternal care in fish that he named the fish in question *Parasilurus Aristotelis*. Aristotle's description of the mouth parts of a sea urchin is so detailed that they are called 'Aristotle's lantern', and his claim that the eggs of the sea urchin are larger at full moon was ridiculed until it was quite recently confirmed for the species he was observing.

But his biological writings were more than a collection of observations. In his *Parts of Animals* and *Generation of Animals* he is concerned with the nature and function of certain organs and seeks to explain them teleologically, that is by assessing what they are 'for'. Nature, he held, 'does nothing in vain' and so he looks for functional explanations for the parts he is considering. But he does not let the theory get in the way of his observations; he is quite prepared to hold, for example, that the colour of eyes might accidental.

Aristotle was also concerned to explain observed differences between animals and he sets out his observations under general headings:

Blooded Animals	Bloodless Animals
Man	Crustacea
Viviparous quadrupeds	Cephalopods
Oviparous quadrupeds and footless animals	Insects
Birds	Testacea
Fishes	

He realized that this system of classification was only one of many that could be drawn up, depending on the criteria, but did suggest to naturalists and philosophers the possibility of a natural scale of living forms from the most primitive to the most developed. In the eighth book of History of Animals, he writes:

Nature gradually advances from things that are without soul (life) to the animals (living things) in such a way that the continuity prevents us from seeing where the boundary comes and from determining from which side of it an intermediate example belongs. First after the lifeless things stand the tribe of plants; and of these one kind of plant differs from another in that it appears to possess a greater share of life; the whole tribe of plants when compared with other objects, seems almost to be endued with soul (life), yet when compared with the tribe of animals it appears to be without soul (life). The advance from plants to animals is continuous, as I have said. Thus, in the sea, there are creatures of which one would be at a loss to say whether they are animals or plants...

[ARISTOTLE, 1991; PP 60-1]

The possession of a soul was the criterion for living matter, but Aristotle suggested that there were three different kinds of soul in the three great classes of living creatures. All have a nutritive, or vegetative soul which guides the intake of food and reproduction. This is the only soul necessary to plants, which do not have to sense and search for their food. The sensitive soul, which all animals have, governs the powers of sense perception, of desire, and of locomotion. Finally man alone has the third soul which has the power of rational thought.

In these speculations Aristotle again moves from the world of scientific observation and theory to that of metaphysics, where he becomes hard to follow. In a chapter on Greek science, we can leave him with his remarks on the elephant's trunk, which show very clearly how much easier Aristotle can be to read than his commentators:

The elephant's nose is unique owing to its enormous size and its extraordinary character. By means of his nose, as if it were a hand, the elephant conveys his food, both solid and fluid, to his mouth; by means of it he tears up trees, by winding it round them. In fact, he uses it for all purposes as if it were a hand. This is because the elephant is a double character; he is a land animal, but he also lives in swamps. He has to get his food from the water; yet he has to breathe because he is a land animal and has blood; owing to his enormous size, however, he cannot transfer himself quickly from the water onto the land as do quite a number of blooded viviparous animals that breathe; hence he has to be equally at home on land and in the water. Some divers when they go down into the sea, provide themselves with a breathing machine, by means of which they can inhale the air from above the surface while they remain for a long time in the water. Nature has provided the elephant with something of the sort by giving him a long nose.   [IBID; Book II]

The first Greek life scientists

Thales (the primal stuff)	**fl. 585**
Anaximander (origins of man)	**fl. 550**
Anaximenes (everything is air)	**fl. 545**
Xenophanes (an honest god's the noblest work of man)	**570–480**
Pythagoras	**fl. 530**
Hippocrates	**460–380**
Aristotle	**384–322**

CHAPTER THREE

Of Gymnastics and Gynaecology

These two words, which sit next to each other in my dictionary, are both directly from the Greek. Both of them have deviated from their original meanings: *gymnos* means 'naked' and so 'gymnastics' included all sports which were performed in the nude. *Gynē* is the Greek word for 'woman' and *logos* here means 'the study of'. We shall deal with both gymnastics and gynaecology in senses close to the Greek originals.

Gymnastics take us to Olympia, the original Olympic Games, which sports were included and how far the Greeks invented the Olympic ideal. Their enthusiasm for athletics was bound up with a fondness for the human body which was celebrated by the greatest sculptors of all time. The Greek word for them is *glyptēs* which survives in our 'glyptic' meaning 'of carving'. Most of the statues are of male nudes and this brings us to the subject of homosexuality and what Greek men got up to with each other. We can then examine how far this male preoccupation with each other pushed women into the background and how much the male domination of Greek society was a male fantasy.

Of all the ancient peoples, the Greeks were the most sporting. The Greek word *athlos* from which we get our 'athletics' is found in all European languages. It is related to *agon*, which means a contest or struggle. The Olympic Games are, in Greek, *Olympiakoi agones*, which many competitors may well feel better expresses the experience of taking part than our tamer word ('game' comes from a root word meaning 'joy' or 'glee'). One of the most characteristic – and to some of us – alarming features of Greek life is that it was based on

67

unremitting competition. In the classical age, all the most important human activities were so organized that Greeks tried to beat each other at them. So Greek art, music, poetry and drama were not only enlarging human awareness and enriching human experience: somebody had to come top. This spirit of rivalry gave zest to the Greek devotion to sport.

There were other reasons for their enthusiasm for athletics. The Greeks were quite unusually preoccupied with the shape of their bodies which, in the heat of the summer months, tended to be on show. Instead of being able, as we are, to pay tailors to create slim hips and pad out broad shoulders, they had to do it the hard way by exercising to produce them naturally. So the Greeks had, if not a general enthusiasm for physical fitness, at least an absence of that sheer distaste for it which is common amongst civilized nations further north. And this, of course, made it less life-threatening to try out a spontaneous two-hundred-yard dash against your friends.

Also the Greeks were trained for warfare from an early age. And warfare meant hand-to-hand combat in which the skills learned on the sports field and the general fitness produced by training could make the difference between life and death.

So, as far back as the records stretch, the Greeks indulged in organized sports. The oldest description of them is in the Iliad, in which, at the Funeral Games for Patroclus, the Greek leaders divert themselves by competing with each other in boxing, wrestling, the race in armour, fencing, discus, javelin, archery and the foot race. In the Odyssey, King Alcinous of the Phaeacians entertains Odysseus with a display of athletics in which his young noblemen contend in the foot race, wrestling and the long jump. Odysseus says at the time he doesn't feel like competing after all he's been through and the young men make the mistake of taunting him. He's obviously only a businessman and no sportsman – if he ever was any good, he's clearly past it. In the style of the best Western hero, Odysseus is driven beyond his patience:

With this he leapt to his feet and, not even troubling to take off his cloak, picked up the *biggest discus of all, a huge weight, more massive by far than the Phaeacians normally used. With one swing he launched it from his mighty hand and the stone hummed on its course. The Phaeacians, lords of the sea and champions of the long oar, cowered down as it hurtled through the air; and, flying smoothly from his hand it overshot the marks of all the other throws.* [HOMER 1991; PP 111-12]

Many small cities in classical times held their own festivals of athletics, but four attracted competitors from all over Greece. These pan-Hellenic games were held at Nemea, a valley in northern Argolis, where they celebrated the victory of Hercules over the Nemean lion and were sacred to Zeus; at Delphi, where they were dedicated to Apollo and called the Pythian games in honour of Apollo Pythios, the priestess who announced the Oracle's answers; at the isthmus of Corinth where they were in honour of Poseidon and at Olympia.

Delphi One day, according to the myths that have an explanation for everything that's important in Greece, Zeus decided to find out the exact centre of the earth. The earth was then shaped like a disc or a saucer, so he sent his messengers with two eagles to opposite sides and ordered them to be released at the same instant. The eagles flew towards each other and then collided, falling to earth locked together. They were buried where they fell, in a single tomb and their image was painted on it with two heads. It became the image of world power and was later used by the emperors of Byzantium. The place where they fell was Delphi, the navel of the earth, the most sacred place.

Here the most famous of oracles gave answers to petitioners from all over Greece to questions that ranged from investment opportunities to the tactics of war or sex. The answers were given by a priestess, called the Pythia, who heard the voice of the god Apollo in the murmuring of a sacred brook, and interpreted by male priests. She was so successful that Delphi became a rich and powerful centre. And here, every four years, were held games in honour of Apollo which were called Pythian, after his priestess.

The exact programme of the Delphic games has not been preserved but, as the athletes took part in the same games every year, it is likely that the same contests were held here as at Olympia. They were so popular that Delphi became gradually covered in hundreds of statues of the victors. The crown was a wreath of laurel.

Isthmia Founded back in the age of mythology, in honour of the god and wrestler Palaemon, who rode into the Isthmus of Corinth on a dolphin's back, the Isthmian Games began as a local celebration which grew to pan-Hellenic status through the power of the city of Corinth, a bustling centre of trade. The Athenians for a time were influential here and put it about that the games had been founded by Theseus to celebrate his having cleared the area of bandits, but the independent Corinthians insisted on their own mythology and commemorated the death of the founder by crowning the winners of the games with wreaths of dried celery.

Nemea The games here were instituted when the seven heroes, marching against the city of Thebes, paused in the valley of Nemea to feed and water their troops. The son of the king was killed by a serpent while they were there and the games were founded in his honour, each of the seven heroes, with the tidiness of tradition, winning one of the seven events. We are not told what these seven events were, but the programme of the games followed that of the Olympics. Because of the funereal origins of the Nemean games, the winner's wreath was of parsley and the ten judges always dressed in dark robes of mourning.

All these games were organized so that at least one pan-Hellenic festival took place each year. Scholars are divided as to the exact order, but there is some agreement that the Olympic games took place in the first year of each Olympiad, the Nemean and the Isthmian in the second year, the Pythian in the third, and the Nemean and Isthmian again in the fourth.

The Olympic Games _____

The Sanctuary of Olympia was not built as a sports stadium. In fact, the stadium itself is a little distance away from the main buildings. The site is magnificent, a level space at the foot of a wooded hill and between two rivers. The Temple of Zeus, which stood in the centre, was a splendid building 20 metres high, 64 metres long and 28 metres wide, with 13 Doric columns along the sides and 6 across the front and back. The statue of Zeus, which stood inside, was the first of the seven wonders of the world. It was carved by Phidias, about seven times life size, and must have sat, rather than stood, inside because standing he would have burst through the roof. Zeus, then, was seated on his throne. In his right hand he held a gold and silver Nike, the symbol of victory, and in his left a sceptre made of all the metals that were known at the time he was sculpted. The frame of the statue was covered in ivory and gold sheets, and the parts of the body not covered by a robe were of ivory. The robe itself, the sandals, the beard and hair were all made of gold and the head was crowned with a silver olive wreath. The throne on which he sat was made of bronze, ebony, gold, ivory and precious stones.

Had the statue survived until the nineteenth century, it would, by now, be safely stowed for the admiration of the citizens of Berlin, London or New York. But it was carted off to Constantinople in 395 AD and was finally destroyed there in the great fire of 475 AD.

There are legends of games having been held at Olympia since prehistoric times, one of them suggesting that they were founded by Zeus himself to commemorate his having fought with and defeated Kronos at that place to win the leadership of the gods. When, in the eighth century BC, Greece was going through a bout of civil wars and the plague, the King of Elis, who ruled over Olympia, asked the Delphic oracle what he could do to bring about a healthy peace. He was told to revive the Olympic games. This he did, starting in 776, and he managed to persuade his neighbours to agree to a Sacred Truce lasting for the month in which the games were celebrated, so that the athletes and their supporters could travel unharmed to Olympia.

The games were held every four years at the time of the second or third full moon following the summer solstice. The athletes would set out during the period of the Sacred Truce for Olympia with their trainers and supporters. One important development from the Homeric games was that these athletes were not necessarily aristocratic; anybody could compete, so long as he was Greek, of a free family and not a criminal. On the way to Olympia, the athletes would bathe in the sacred spring of Pieria and make sacrifices there. They had to train for at least ten months at their homes before the games and then for a further month, under the supervision of the Olympic judges, at Olympia.

The first day of the festival was taken up by oaths and registration. All the athletes had to swear in front of the statue of Zeus that they had trained for ten months and that they would compete fairly and abide by the rules. Their fathers, brothers and trainers would then swear that they had all trained together for the ten-month period and that the athletes were entitled to take part in the games. Then the judges would come forward and take oaths to be impartial. Then there was a magnificent and long-drawn-out procession, forerunner of so many opening ceremonies, with the judges in flowing purple robes followed by the sleekly-oiled athletes marching around the Stadium while the proclamation was made to all Greeks that the Games were beginning.

On the second day the horse and chariot races were held in the Hippodrome and afterwards the Pentathlon back in the Stadium.

The third day was the most magnificent, in which the judges, the athletes, the city dignitaries, and delegates from all the Greek cities marched to the temple of Zeus and stood around the great altar whilst a hundred oxen were sacrificed to the god. After this they went back to the Stadium where the track events were held.

On the fourth day the really punishing events took place: boxing, wrestling and the races in heavy armour.

And finally, on the fifth and last day, the prizes were awarded in the entrance of the temple of Zeus, where, on a table of ivory and gold, were the garlands of wild olives. The judges crowned the victors and then held a great feast in their honour, to which were invited all the delegates from the Greek cities and the distinguished visitors. The Olympic Games attracted public figures: great politicians, famous generals, philosophers, poets and intellectuals were all to be seen there. Plato and Aristotle were regulars, and Herodotus even read there extracts from his history of the Greek victories over the Persians, moving Thucydides, who heard them, to decide to be a historian himself.

The most ancient athletic event was the Stade race, that is a flat race the length of the stadium, which is 192.25 metres, or close enough to a 200-yard dash. The starting line can still be seen at Olympia, a series of marble blocks set into the ground with grooves in them against which the runners set their toes and, possibly, their hands – though the evidence from pottery pictures suggests they started standing up. This was the only event until 728 BC when the games expanded. The *diaulos*, close to the quarter mile, was two lengths of the stadium and the *dolichos* or long haul was 24 stades (192.4m × 24), or close to the three-mile race. The runners ran naked, their bodies coated with oil, and the vase paintings seem to suggest that the earlier sprinters were short and thick-set while the long-distance runners who came later were taller and thinner.

There was also a race in armour in honour of the heroes of old who raced outside the walls of Troy, and a torch race, a relay in which blazing torches were passed from hand to hand and the prize went to the team which first arrived with a still-lighted torch at the altar of the god. This last seems to have been more a religious than an athletic event and commemorated the great occasion in the history of the human race when Prometheus stole fire from the gods and brought it down to earth.

Wrestling was the oldest of all sports. It was always a favourite among the aristocrats. Homer has a lively description of a contest between Odysseus himself – the cunning one – and the huge but stolid Ajax in Book 23 of the *Iliad*. The prize for the winner was a great tripod to stand over the fire, valued at twelve oxen, while the loser had to content himself with a woman skilled in handicrafts and worth only four:

These two then belted themselves and walked out into the centre of the gathering. They gripped each other in the embrace of their massive arms like the rafters which a skilled builder fits locking together in the roof of a high house to keep out the force of the winds. Their backs cracked under the tight pressure of powerful hands and the sweat ran pouring down. Weals swelling red with blood sprang up all over their sides and shoulders as they struggled hard for victory and the prize of the crafted tripod. [HOMER, Iliad 1987; p 388]

The contest was declared a draw. In classical times, children were trained for wrestling at school where they began by digging over the ground with a spade to soften it. Then they faced each other in pairs and, with heads down and arms outstretched, tried to get a grip on each other by the neck or the waist to execute a throw. The object was to unbalance your opponent and throw him to the ground while you remained standing. Three falls brought victory. The different grips and throws were taught and set out in school manuals, and a large technical vocabulary developed which writers put to metaphorical and sometimes erotic use.

At the Olympics the contests took place in a shallow pit dug into the stadium and the contestants relied mainly on strength and bulk. The most well known wrestler was Milon, a pupil of Pythagoras, from Croton in southern Italy, who took the prize six times at the Olympics and six times at the Pythian games. He was famous for having once paraded around the stadium with a live young bull on his shoulders which he then killed and ate in a single day. He died ingloriously when, having split open a tree with his bare hands, his fingers were caught in the cleft and he was eaten by a pack of wolves.

Boxing was another ancient sport recorded in Homer. The hands were bound with leather thongs, more to protect the knuckles than to hurt the opponent – though of course the Romans later thought up the idea of loading the thongs with pieces of iron and metal spikes to add to the spectators' enjoyment. Boxing opponents were chosen by lot and, as there were no timed rounds at the Olympic games, stamina was important. But, as there were no classifications of bouts by weight, the bigger and heavier men tended to win. That the fights were more than slugging matches is indicated by both the vase painters and in the literature, and the third-century poet Theocritus has a description of a boxing match in which agility and skill are pitted against brute strength, reminiscent of the famous bout between Gentleman Jim Corbett and John L. Sullivan for the heavyweight championship of the world:

Then Amycus came on furiously, making play with both hands; but Pollux hit him on the point of the chin as he charged, making him madder, and the giant tried to mix it, laying on with all his might and going in with head down ... But the son of Zeus dodged, now this side now that, and hit him with one-twos and brought him up short for all his strength. Like a drunken man he reeled under the hero's blows and spat out red blood while all the princes shouted together as they saw the ugly bruises about his mouth and jaws, and his eyes half closed by puffy flesh. Next Pollux began to tease him, feinting on every side and, at last, seeing he was all confused, he got in a smashing blow just on the bridge of the nose beneath the eyebrows and laid bare the bone of his forehead. The giant fell, stretched on his back amongst the flowers; but he got up again and the fight went on fiercely. They mauled each other hard, laying on with the weighted thongs, but the giant concentrated on body blows to the chest and neck while Pollux, the invincible, kept smashing his opponent's face with cruel blows.   [THEOCRITUS, Idyll xxii, 87-111]

Jumping at the Olympics was confined to the long jump which was performed with the help of jumping weights called *halteres*, small dumb-bells made of stone or lead and weighing between two and ten pounds. They were carried, one in each hand, and swung forward at the take-off point to give added impetus. The athletes of our own time have tried them out in both running and standing jumps. In the running jump they are a hindrance, but they do seem to help in the standing jump and so the assumption is that this is the way the Greeks did it. The best of three jumps was taken.

The javelin was a light stick of wood, the thickness of a finger and the height of a man, usually without a point but weighted at the tip. At its centre of gravity the Greeks fastened a thin leather thong about 60 cm (2 ft) long with a ring at the end which the athlete slipped over the index and middle fingers of his throwing hand. This very much increases the possible distance though its use takes some practice and, of course, it is more suitable for games than for hunting or war.

The discus was a flat circle of bronze, varying in size between two and eight pounds, and was thrown from behind a U-shaped base, marked at the front and sides. It was usually covered in sand so that it would not slip through the fingers in the complicated gyrations of the throw. In the earliest times, the discus seems to have been made of stone and a series of them of different sizes and weights were used (see the story of Odysseus above, pages 68–9). First the athlete would raise the discus in both hands above his head. Then he would lean forwards and suddenly swing round from left to right, his discus arm describing a wide circle to increase the centrifugal force. It is not easy to see how the elegant young man in the famous Discobolos statue by Myron, with his left toes scraping along the ground, could have done very well – indeed, as someone observed, he is clearly about to fall on his nose – but the statue is there to celebrate an aesthetic harmony and not to teach athletics.

The race in full armour was restricted to the men who could afford it and so possibly marked the emergence in the sporting arena of the middle class. It must have been a taxing event because the full armour of a Greek hoplite needed a strong man to stand, let alone run, in it. It consisted of four pieces: the helmet, the cuirass, the greaves and the shield. The helmet was made of beaten metal and had detachable pieces protecting the neck, cheeks, and nose. The cuirass, in its early form, consisted of two bronze plates roughly shaped to fit the body and fastened at the sides and shoulders and the greaves were thin sheets of bronze shaped to fit the leg and held on by their own elasticity. Some went only to the knee, but others covered the thigh and there were ankle pads to prevent the bottom edge of the greave from chafing the foot. The Homeric shield had been 'great as a tower' and tall enough to protect a man from head to foot, but, by the fifth century, the oval shield about a metre (three feet) long had become the most common. The inside of the shield had a metal or leather strap through which to pass the left arm and one or two grips of cord or leather at the edge to give a firm grip. It was a heavy implement, designed to withstand the shock of direct blows and needed a strong arm to keep it up. So the race in armour was known as 'The Shield' and, although the competitors cannot have achieved great speeds, the colour of the event made it a favourite among vase painters.

The chariot race was for the aristocratic; few men outside the old families could afford to keep horses. It was the noisiest, dustiest, most dangerous and exciting event of the games and the competitors added to the glamour of the occasion by being distinguished heroes, generals, or even tyrants. The chariot had two wheels and was pulled by a team of four horses, yoked in pairs, one to the frame of the chariot and the other, on long traces, running in front. The skill was to control the outriders so that they would come close in to the turning post and avoid the time-wasting wide swing before heading back down the straight. The race took twelve complete laps of the stadium with 180-degree turns at each end and it must have been a rare event for all the competitors to finish it.

Homer has a magnificent description of a chariot race in book 23 of the *Iliad*, which is one of the most exciting sports commentaries ever written. At the start, the five chariots are in line, having drawn lots for position.

Achilles points out to the charioteers the turning post where an umpire is stationed to make sure that they all go round it. Then the signal is given:

At the same moment they all raised their whips over their horses and brought the lash down on them, and shouted them forward with urgent commands. At once they were speeding over the plain, far from the ships. Under their chests the dust rose and hung like a cloud or a thunderhead, and their manes streamed back in the rush of the wind. The chariots would bounce at one moment close to the nourishing earth and then be leaping in the air off the ground. The heart of every driver standing in his car beat hard as he strained for victory; each man called to his own horses and they flew on raising the dust over the plain. [HOMER, Iliad 23 1987; P380]

Half-way round the track, the leading chariot is driven by Eumelos, an outstanding horseman, when the yoke breaks:

His mares ran off the road, the shaft dropped to the ground, and Eumelos himself was tumbled out of the chariot beside the wheel. The skin was ripped from elbows, mouth and nose, and his forehead smashed in over his eyebrows; his eyes filled with tears and his strong voice was blocked.   [IBID; P 381]

The spectators at the winning post, straining their eyes over the plain, can see only a great cloud of dust and start laying bets with each other as to who will first come out of it when:

the son of Tydeus came driving in towards them, very close now, all the time lashing his horses on with the whip swung full from the shoulder; and they bounded on for him, springing speedily on their way. A constant spray of dust rained on their driver, and the chariot with its overlays of gold and tin came whirling at the heels of the fast running horses, and there was hardly any track made by the wheel rims in the fine dust behind them as they flew speeding on. Diomedes pulled up in the middle of the gathering with a thick sweat welling on the neck and chest of his horses and dripping to the ground. He himself jumped down from his glittering chariot and leant his whip against the yoke.   [IBID; P 383]

It may well be significant that we have few sporting records from the 1200 years of the old Olympics. The Greeks were interested in who won, but not in how well he did. Of course there were no accurate ways of timing the sprints, but the long jump, javelin and discus had to be measured and it would have been easy to start a table of Olympic records starting from the year 776. But there's no honour for a Greek in beating a measuring stick. The athletes were there, under the eyes of the spectators, in search of the celebrity which came from defeating opposition on the day, not advancing human achievement by jumping or throwing that few inches further. So that the Olympic ideal as we celebrate it today is perfectly Greek in the sense that athletes pledge themselves to compete fairly, but it is almost entirely English if we interpret it as meaning that playing the game is more important than winning. The idea of being a 'good loser' would have mystified the Greeks.

Only the winners mattered at Olympia. Although their prize at the games was just the simple crown of wild olive leaves, they were feasted on their return home, their family and their city became famous and they were given free meals for life at the public feasts. There is even a record of a city wall having been broken down so that the hero's chariot might enter where no previous foot had trod. The Victory Odes of Pindar celebrate success in games as never before or since: at the instant of the victor's triumph, he is elevated in a flash to a semi-divine status which is the final justification for human existence. The athletes who came second returned in disgrace. Even today, Greeks hate to come second, as anybody will testify who has tried in Greece to queue for a ferry or a postage stamp.

Sculpture

One effect of this public adulation for the successful sportsman was a multitude of commemorative statues of naked athletes. These not only served as tributes to the victors, they celebrated the beauty of the male form. The Greeks were the first people to indulge in such a celebration.

Greek sculpture can be – quite literally – breathtaking. To stand quietly in front of one of the great masterpieces and feel its impact today is an experience close to that of hearing great music. But the impact has to be direct, the experience personally felt. And so much has been written about Greek art that it is almost impossible to stand in front of any Greek statue today without having picked up somebody's opinion about how we should be feeling. So Greek sculpture, for the aesthetically anxious, can be a minefield, because no sooner has one critic sung the praises of a statue than up pops another claiming it is an inferior Roman copy.

There is a moral tale for all of us in the most famous of all Apollos, the Apollo Belvedere. This had been, by the beginning of the nineteenth century, for three hundred years one of the most famous pieces of sculpture in the world. It was described by the German art critic Winckelmann as the Ultimate:

The eternal spring of youth covers the perfect manliness of the body ... If God should be pleased to reveal himself in such a shape all the world would worship at his feet ... It is the highest ideal of art among all the works of antiquity. Enter, O reader, with your spirit into this kingdom of beauty incarnate, and there seek to create for yourself the images of the divine nature. [QUOTED CLARK 1957; P45]

Byron rhapsodized about the statue and wrote of it:

... the Lord of the unerring bow
The God of life, and poesy and light —
The Sun in human limbs array'd, and brow
All radiant from his triumph in the fight ...
The shaft hath just been shot — the arrow bright
With an immortal's vengeance; in his eye
And nostril beautiful disdain, and might
And majesty, flash their full lightenings by,
Developing in that one glance the Deity.
[Childe Harold canto 4, cixi]

His biographer, Thomas Moore, tactfully compared Byron's own features, with the beautifully disdainful nostrils, to those of the Apollo Belvedere, which would have pleased the poet, had he been alive. But the statue always put me in mind of a Principal Boy in pantomime, a role traditionally taken by a strapping girl. You feel he's about to step up and lead the chorus in a high kicking routine; the Apollo Belvedere would be more at home on a theatre organ than a Greek temple and whatever ecstasies he inspired in Winckelmann seems to me inescapably high camp. Fortunately, Kenneth Clark agrees and:

can only imagine that for three hundred years the Apollo satisfied the same sort of uncritical hunger which was later to crave for the plumes and pinnacles of romanticism; and as long as it did so, the eye could overlook weak structure and slack surfaces which, to the aesthetic of pure sensibility, annul its other qualities. In no other famous work of art, perhaps, are idea and execution more distressingly divorced ... [CLARK 1957; P45]

The reassuring outcome of a fracas among the experts is that the rest of us can feel free to admire where admiration is called for; in looking at Greek sculpture it frequently is.

There is another point. Many admirers of Greek sculptures have stressed that the beauty they express is the result of balance, harmony and proportion. If the contemplation and admiration of this beauty are disturbed by thoughts appropriate to the subject matter – in other words, if the statues are found to be in the slightest degree sexually arousing – the pure appreciation of their true qualities is tarnished. Professor Samuel Alexander, in his book *Beauty and other forms of Value*, writes: 'If the nude is so treated that it raises in the spectator ideas or desires appropriate to the material subject, it is false art and bad morals' [p 127]. The point was stressed by a classics master who taught Lawrence Durrell and had the habit of producing before the boys a tattered photograph of the Venus de Milo, banging the desk and shouting: 'What do you think they were trying to do? Make us tingle with lust? Certainly not! They were asking themselves what beauty is, and whether it lies in proportion' [quoted in Leckie 1989; p lii]. I remembered this story when touring the Greek sites on a cruise ship. The ship's doctor told me that, in the old days, after their visits to the exhibitions of male sculptures, it was the practice to shell out bromides to the unaccompanied ladies who found the nude statues 'emotionally disturbing'. This was not because their aesthetic sensibilities had been overstimulated, but because they had been assailed by 'thoughts appropriate to the subject matter'. Well, on the authority of Sir Kenneth Clark, tingling is not only allowed, it's commendable. All these high-minded theories about the purity of the nude and the glacial aesthetic satisfaction that comes from the contemplation of true proportion are contrary to experience. 'No nude', he protests, 'however abstract, should fail to arouse in the spectator some vestige of erotic feeling ... and if it does not do so, it is bad art and false morals.' [Clark 1957; p 6]

The earliest statues which have survived are of the *kouros*, or youth. They date from the sixth century and are what you might expect to find along the banks of the Nile or in the Egyptian galleries of our museums. They stand four square, body formally erect without a turn or twist, looking straight ahead and with their arms at their sides, occasionally slightly bent, and hands lightly clenched with thumbs forward. The hair falls over the shoulder in formal plaits and the left foot is slightly forward. These statues are all somehow disengaged from the world around them; they have a monumental timeless quality like the guardians of Egyptian temples. But there are differences in Greece. Normally the Egyptian statues wear kilts, but the kouroi are naked; sometimes the Egyptians are bearded, the Greeks never; and often the Greeks have just the hint of a smile about the lips which gives them a faintly self-satisfied air quite foreign to the solemn Egyptians.

When these statues were first discovered they were called Apollos and indeed early cult statues to the god did survive in Delos and Miletus, but these kouroi seem to represent nothing beyond themselves; they may have been carved in commemoration of the dead, but they did not represent individuals, simply a stark and unvaried youth.

There is one highly individual surviving statue from the Acropolis dated around 575–550; it is Rhombus, an Athenian citizen whose name appears on the pedestal. But although he stands like a kouros, he has a beard and a cloak and carries a calf on his shoulders. Another striking statue from the same place but about a generation younger is the Peplos Kore, so called because the young girl or kore portrayed wears a woollen peplos or veil over her chiton. She has a compelling face: high cheekbones, almond eyes and a mouth whose corners pucker into a faint smile.

There are two famous and different statues which extend the manner of the simple kouros. One is the Charioteer at Delphi, a life-size bronze figure probably erected as a votive offering after a race. It stands expressionless with one arm extended holding the reins, the body hidden in the folds of a garment that stretches from shoulder to ankle. Photographs can never capture the atmosphere of serenity that surrounds this figure, which even extends out into the maelstrom of the Delphi museum in midsummer.

The Omphalos Apollo, of which a good copy survives in the Athens museum, dates from near the middle of the fifth century and shows the final stage in the relaxation of the standing male figure from the earliest kouroi. Now the weight is thrown on to one leg and the line of the shoulders, hips and knees is no longer horizontal but alternating up and down.

One of the finest of surviving bronze statues is that of the striding Poseidon, or Zeus, probably made at about the same time. It was found in the sea off Cape Artemision, probably part of a shipment of statues being carried out of the country. Today it stands in the National Museum in Athens, left foot forward, left arm extended, right arm drawn back ready to hurl a weapon which has not survived. If it was a trident, the figure represents Poseidon, if a thunderbolt, it must be Zeus. The noble head has a sharp, spade-like beard and immense vigour.

But the sculptor who became most celebrated for arrested movement was Myron who, in the mid-fifth century, lived in Athens and experimented with different poses showing athletes about to begin, or arrested suddenly in the process of violent action. His most famous statue is the Discobolos: 'one of those inexplicable leaps by which genius has advanced the range of human achievement' [Clark 1957; p 167]. An athlete who has just transferred the discus from both hands to his right one prepares to pivot suddenly about the right foot and hurl it. The pose is convincing enough, thought I have to admit that when I taught sports for a time at a London boys' school, and tried to imitate this posture in the discus lessons, I kept falling over. Perhaps the fault was mine rather than the sculptor's, but the feet do seem rather close together for a secure balance. The figure is so arranged that it is most satisfactorily seen from the front as is his other work Marsyas where the bearded satyr is starting back from something on the ground in front of him. This was possibly one of a group of two in which the goddess Athena, having tried to play the flute, discovers that it distorts her face and throws the instrument in disgust to the ground. Marsyas was fated to pick it up and challenge Apollo to a contest which he lost and suffered the penalty of being flayed alive.

Nothing original survives of the work of the most influential of sculptors of this time, Polyclitus, famous for sculpting the human male nude, not as he observed it, but as it ought to be. Polyclitus worked out certain rules which he decided must be followed to achieve perfection of form. There are a few surviving fragments of his instructions, such as seven and a half heads should equal one body, but there are no exemplars from his hand by which his principles can be judged. A Roman copy in marble of the Spearbearer, or Doryphoros, survives. But Roman copies, insensitively executed, are particularly likely to fail an artist who said that 'a well-made work is the result of numerous calculations carried to within a hair's breadth'. There is a story that Polyclitus demonstrated the importance of his canon in a very practical way. He made two statues of the same model, one in a popular and naturalistic style, the other according to the strict canons of his art. He then invited all his friends to suggest improvements to the first one and amended it to take account of all they suggested. Finally he exhibited the two statues to the general ridicule of the first and the admiration of the second. This he saw as a practical demonstration of the philosophical principle that beauty was a matter of ratio and proportion and so, ultimately, of mathematics.

The second statue of Polyclitus which has survived in numerous copies is his Diadumenos, which portrays a youth binding a fillet around his head. Again the proportions are the same – slightly heavier with more developed muscles than the works of Myron – and the overall effect is one of a placid balance rather than arrested motion.

The Greeks thought highly of Polyclitus but said that though he had created the perfectly balanced man he had not the gift of creating a god. That was given to Phidias. No sculptor was more celebrated than the creator of the great statue of Zeus at Olympia. He was an Athenian and made his reputation from two memorials to the battle of Marathon, one a bronze group at Delphi, and the other a 9-metre (30-feet) high statue of Athena Promachos said to have been made in bronze from the weapons of the Persians taken at Marathon, though it's more likely that the sale of those weapons helped pay for it. This stood high on the Sacred Way to the east door of the Parthenon and seems to have been a landmark in the style of the Statue of Liberty from about 470 onwards. It has survived only in small representations on Roman coins. But Phidias became the friend of Pericles and was put in charge of the sculptures of the Parthenon. His style fitted perfectly the monument to Greek superiority: his statues are marked by an aloof, serene majesty perhaps best displayed in the

Apollo who stands on the West pediment, rebuking the bestial fury of the centaurs.

Phidias paid for his friendship with Pericles by being involved in legal proceedings for embezzlement brought by political enemies who claimed that he had used up some of the gold given to him for the statues. He fled to Olympia, where his workshop and a cup bearing his name have been excavated. There he executed the great statue of Zeus in gold and ivory which became the first of the seven wonders of the ancient world. It was apparently a portrayal of Zeus the 'Kindly One', its expression one of Olympic serenity and infinite calm. The Roman rhetorician Quintilian, who saw it in the first century AD, wrote that its beauty 'could be said to have added something to traditional religion, so adequate to the divine nature was the majesty of his work' [quoted Richter 1974; p 118].

In 1972, in the sea off Riace in Calabria, south-western Italy, two bronze statues were discovered. They are about six feet tall, naked, standing, and bearded. Nothing so startling has survived from the whole classical period. The younger man has long curling hair encircled by a band which was probably of gold; his nipples are of copper, his teeth are silver. He stands in a swaggering pose, chest thrown out, heavily muscled. His left arm probably held a shield and his right a sword, ready to take on all comers. The older has a surviving eye of ivory and glass paste, a fuller beard and the same heavy build and defiant stance. Their workmanship suggests that they were from the same workshop, made at the same time.

As yet no art historian has given a firm attribution to them, though some have suggested that they are part of a group of figures sculpted by Phidias and dedicated by the Athenians at Delphi to celebrate their victory at the battle of Marathon. They are thought to date from the early part of the fifth century but their details would have shocked the artists of that period who, we have been told by the critics, were in search of the ideal of the human figure and not given to realistic representations. They are of such superb quality that they represent the climax of sculpture of classical Greece, and Ernst Gombrich comments on them that:

like all great works of art these new finds refute the dogmas of critics and show triumphantly that the more we generalise about art the more likely we are to go wrong.

[GOMBRICH 1991; P 501]

As Phidias and Polyclitus had dominated the art of the fifth century, so Praxiteles of Athens, Skopas of Paros, and Lysippus of Sikyon dominated the fourth.

Praxiteles, an Athenian, was commissioned by the people of the island of Kos to sculpt an Aphrodite in about the year 340. It was a voluptuous figure, entirely naked with swelling buttocks and adolescent breasts, the left hand draping her robe over an urn, as she prepares to get into a bath, the right hand affecting to conceal but drawing attention to her genital area. The figure, said to have been taken from a living model, Phryne, an Athenian prostitute, was so compellingly erotic that a workman, the story goes, tried to mount it and this was too much for the people of Kos. They refused to accept it and it was placed in an open shrine, to be viewed from all sides, set up high on a hillside overlooking Cnidos and became known as the Aphrodite of Cnidos. She must have been well worth the climb. The elder Pliny described her as the finest statue ever made anywhere in the world. He obviously was not averse to tingling as this Aphrodite seems to combine as no other work of art the erotic with the sacred:

Perhaps no religion ever again incorporated physical passion as calmly, as sweetly and as naturally so that all who saw her felt that the instincts they shared with the beasts they also shared with the gods. [CLARK 1957; P 74]

It's no surprise that the Aphrodites of Cnidos failed to survive the Roman occupation. We can know it today only through copies, of which thousands were made in ancient times. Forty-nine full-sized ones survive. In looking at them it helps to remember the translucent beauty of the Hermes at Olympia which must once have been hers.

This, the only surviving statue of Praxiteles – though there are those who claim it to be a copy – shows the god Hermes carrying the infant Dionysus. Dionysus had been born to Semele, daughter of the King of Thebes who unwisely asked Zeus, his father, to appear before her in all his divine glory. Zeus did so and she was immediately burned to a cinder. So Hermes was given the job of taking the infant Dionysus to be looked after by the Nymphs of Boeotia. He is on his way there but, tired, stops to rest by a tree. He leans firmly on his right foot, the left one is relaxed as he turns to the left. His cloak is draped over the treetrunk on which he is leaning. The statue is made from a soft, smooth Parian marble, giving the figure a sensuous, even effeminate look. Hermes has a noble, youthful, heroic face with a hint of a smile, as he holds the child in the crook of his left arm and attracts its attention with a bunch of grapes held in the right hand, now missing. The overall impression of the statue – and it is a powerful one today as we can see it from all sides in its own room at Olympia, is one of a dreamy, sensuous grace.

Skopas was more interested in the pathos and suffering of the human condition. He revelled in dramatic scenes and since writhing and ecstatic bodies tend to be inherently unstable, his best work is found in friezes: the Calydonian boar hunt and the Battle of the Caicus with quivering bodies vibrating with Dionysiac passion. He was the architect of the temple of Athena at Tegea and the sculpture there, of which fragments have survived, was probably his. These are massive heads with thick-set features and deep-set eyes reflecting the eternal conflicts of the gods. They inhabit a world far removed from that of Praxiteles and remind us that there were Greeks driven by irrational forces even whilst others were using measuring sticks in the quest for eternal beauty. He is said to have worked on the Mausoleum of Halicarnassus, one of the seven wonders of the world, but nobody is absolutely sure which of the few extant reliefs can be attributed to him. There is a youth with crossed legs leaning on a pillar with a goose at his feet called Pothos or Longing, of which the Romans made many copies, but these convey little more than a Victorian sentimental cloying sweetness.

Lysippus was a younger contemporary of Skopas and Praxiteles who broke away from the strict canons of his master to portray the human body, not as it should be but as it frequently was. Pliny records that, when asked who his masters were, Lysippus pointed to a crowd of men in a street. His Agias has survived in a marble copy, found at Delphi and thought to have been made at the same time as the bronze original. It is a fine statue of a particular athlete – as opposed to the ideal Athlete – whose head is smaller and legs slightly longer than the athlete which Polyclitus designed. The attribution to Lysippus has been challenged and we are on safer ground with another, similarly proportioned figure, the Apoxyomenos, or Youth Scraping Himself Off, which is in the Vatican. This has a novel pose in which the weight is neither set on both feet nor resting on one, but being transferred from one foot to the other, giving a sense of lightness and movement. The arms are stretched out in front so that the statue occupies more depth than its predecessors and can be seen to advantage from a wider range of angles.

Lysippus met Alexander the Great and became the official sculptor of the Emperor, whom he portrayed with leonine hair and great moist eyes, looking forward to the royal sculptures of the Hellenistic period which are interesting to historians but give little pleasure to anybody else.

That the Greeks excelled in sculpting the bodies of their male athletes is connected with their second best known activity.

Homosexuality

We must now turn fearlessly to a sensitive topic which brought many a blush to the cheek of the Master of Balliol, Benjamin Jowett, in his translations from the Greek and caused his decorous pen to falter. It has disturbed many an admirer of the Greeks to think that the well-muscled young men so magnificently sculpted were completely uninterested in any of the young maidens in *draperie mouille* who accompanied them – because they actually preferred each other.

The sixth-century lyric poet Anakreon, whose surviving work is mainly taken up with enjoying the sensual pleasures of life and who was, not surprisingly, much admired by Lord Byron in the translation by his friend Thomas Moore, wrote the much-quoted lines:

Boy with the virginal eyes,
I seek you but you do not hear,
for you know that you are
the charioteer of my soul.

And two of the best attested poems of the philosopher Plato are in praise of the boy Aster:

My Star, are you star-gazing? I wish that I could be
The sky, with all its eyes, to gaze on you...

You were the morning star shining on the living:
But now, in death, your evening star lights up the dead.

Greek homosexuality has always had its admirers in modern times. From the circle of Oscar Wilde and Yellow Book dandyism, through the aesthetes of the Bloomsbury group to the Gay Liberationists of our own days there have been those who proclaimed that the Greeks were the noble savages of an Arcadian past, living an uninhibited life of natural sexual freedom before the grey shadow of Christianity fell across their world. That the Greeks should have recognized the homosexual orientation as healthy, spontaneous and instinctive has been held to be yet another example of their enlightened attitudes to life. But what exactly were those attitudes? Did they really believe that homosexual relationships were more desirable than heterosexual ones? How widespread were they? And what, exactly, did Greek homosexuals do to and with each other?

These are questions which have been fudged for many years, the evidence remaining in the decent obscurity of a dead language. Scholars, when confronted by evidence that the founders of Western Civilization had what they might have called sexually aberrant tendencies, have tended to look the other way. R. W. Livingstone, for all his devotion to Greek studies, enjoins: 'It is at times chastening to remember, as it is generally better to forget, that many of the most graceful Greek vases are offerings dedicated to unnatural vice' [Livingstone 1912; pp 25–6].

Fortunately these questions have been intrepidly tackled by one of the foremost classicists of our own age: Sir Kenneth Dover, whose lack of inhibition in this field causes his book *Greek Homosexuality* to be locked away in the safe of the London Library. In it, he points out that much of the writing on this subject is from scholars who are *parti pris* in the sense that they are either scandalized by what they have to reveal or wish to enlist the Greeks to support their own sexual predilections. Sir Kenneth is unusual in being able to confess himself unshockable in the observation and discussion of the pleasure people have been able to take from their genitals, and is clearly the ideal man to tackle the subject.

But what he reveals is of small comfort to the gay lobby. Although classical Greeks regarded the desire of adult males for sexual pleasure from handsome youths as perfectly normal, Dover makes it quite clear that 'the reciprocal desire of partners belonging to the same age category is virtually unknown in Greek homosexuality'. The older Greek men were all for trying it on, and occasionally having it off, with good-looking young men; but the young men did not, it seems, either fancy each other or enjoy what they had to put up with from their elders.

Both in the literature and in the pottery decorations which are the best source material, often depicting what men got up to with each other with an attention to detail that would stop the conversation in any dinner party today, it is clear that there is a distinction between the *erastes*, the lover, the active, older partner, and the *eromenos*, the beloved, or passive and younger partner. The older man is often portrayed fondling the genitals of the younger; he often has an erection, the younger never does. When copulation took place it was intercrural, or between the thighs. A young man who allowed anal penetration was scorned as letting himself be used as a woman. There were male prostitutes who allowed this, but it was contrary to the law and any Athenian found guilty of it could be deprived of citizenship.

So the older men were expected to chase the youths who were expected to resist them – just as in heterosexual relationships. But an important distinction between Greek homosexual practices and those of our own time is that the Greeks sought genital pleasure where they could find it, having no inherited religious prohibition of homosexuality, and did not think of homosexual acts as necessarily indicating a fundamental orientation of sexuality. They enjoyed girls and they enjoyed young men, and would have found it curious to suggest that one precludes the other.

There were indeed Greek gays who 'came out' in public and Aristophanes has a few laughs at their expense but generally the leisured classes could be described, if the word existed, as ambiphallic.

There is a delightful description of the seduction techniques of the Greek bent on homosexual pleasure in the most quoted book on the subject, Plato's Symposium. As Plato was, as we'll discuss later, much given to irony, the story he tells is unlikely to have a factual basis; indeed, because the narrator is Alcibiades, one of the best-looking young men in Athens, and the man he is trying to seduce is Socrates, one of the worst-looking old ones, the situation is clearly meant to be comic:

As I was saying, we were alone together and I was enjoying the thought that we should soon embark on the kind of talk a lover has when he is alone with his beloved. Not a bit of it; he spent the day with me in his usual kind of talk and then he went off and left me. After that I asked him to train with me in the gymnasium, which he did, and I hoped to get somewhere. But, although we exercised and wrestled together, often with nobody else present, I need hardly say that I got no further . . . So I invited him to dinner with me, behaving as if I were the lover and he the beloved. He did not accept in a hurry but, in the end, I persuaded him. The first time he came, he wanted to leave immediately after dinner and I was ashamed and let him go. But I tried again and this time kept him in conversation far into the night, and when he wanted to go I pretended it was too late and managed to force him to stay. So he lay down on the couch next to mine, on which he had dined. There was nobody else sleeping in the room except the two of us, and so far the story could properly be told to anyone . . .   [PLATO, Symposium]

And the story ends by Alcibiades offering himself to Socrates and getting, in return, a philosophical lecture.

The Symposium was written for and about the upper-class intellectuals in Athens and its attitudes need not represent those current in Athenian society at large. To what extent they did so is still heatedly contested by scholars of various sexual predilections. A summary of the situation can safely be left to the most balanced of them all, Sir Kenneth Dover:

The Greeks neither inherited nor developed a belief that a divine power had revealed to mankind a code of laws for the regulation of sexual behaviour; they had no religious institution possessed of the authority to enforce sexual prohibitions. Confronted by cultures older and richer and more elaborate than theirs, the Greeks felt free to select, adapt, develop and — above all — innovate. Fragmented as they were into tiny political units, they were constantly aware of the extent to which morals and manners are local. This awareness also disposed them to enjoy the products of their own inventiveness and to attribute a similar enjoyment to their deities and heroes.   [DOVER 1978; P 203]

Women

When we come to consider the position of women in Greek society, it's worth remembering that all the written evidence comes from men; and that the scholars who have, in the past, interpreted that evidence for us were often the bachelor dons who occupied Fellowships at our older universities. Set against this the fact that much recent research has been inspired by the ebullient feminism of our own age and, as the Greeks would have said, we're about to steer between Scylla and Charybdis.

Before sticking a toe into these troubled waters, perhaps I can mention a personal experience which may be relevant. For fifteen years I lived as a colonial administrator in the Fiji Islands where, even more than in classical Greece, the women had a raw deal. They took no part in public life; all the important decisions were taken by the men after lengthy public debates from which women were excluded; the great ceremonies which had to go on before anybody could talk about anything important were performed by the men; at the feasts which followed, the men ate first, served by the women who would then eat whatever was left. The Fijian chief usually had several wives and they used to insist, before the arrival of the missionaries, if their husbands died, on being strangled with a pandanus rope so they could accompany him in the afterlife. Everybody agreed – planters, missionaries, colonial administrators and anthropologists – that the women's traditional role in Fiji was a submissive and obedient, not to say degraded one. Just like their role in ancient Greece.

It was only after some years that I came to suspect that this role might just be for public consumption. This is how the light dawned. We, that is the men of a village and I, would debate the need for some sort of public work – a new roof for the church, say, or a lavatory block for the school. After a kava ceremony lasting an hour and a half there would be speeches from the older men on the wisdom, or lack of it, in the proposal; sometimes the younger men would chip in with comments as they were the ones likely to have to do the work; we would talk about the availability and cost of the materials, the need to arrange a work programme to avoid other communal obligations, and we would eventually, after a debate of three or four hours, reach a final decision. Then we, that is the men and I, would sit down for a meal which the women had been preparing during the long public debate. We would sit on the long mat and be served taro and fish and yams and sweet potatoes by the women who sat behind us and only interfered to bring on more food or water. Then I would go back home. And nothing would happen.

When nothing went on happening as the months passed, I would go back to the village to ask why. Usually there were plausible excuses but then, occasionally, I would hear a whisper that the women of the village just didn't think whatever we men had decided on was a good idea. And some of the men of the village who, over the years, became friends, began to admit in confidence that, whatever they decided at a public meeting, they still had to go home afterwards; and that home with a discontented wife was no place to be.

So, when I came to learn about the Greeks, and I read that the women were merely slaves without legal rights, to be given in marriage by their parents, kept in seclusion in their houses, not allowed to own property or speak in public debate, and generally morally, socially and intellectually of no account, I started to hear warning bells. Because Greek men, too, had to go home.

Perhaps it's worth noticing that, of the twelve celebrated deities of Mount Olympus, half were female. And none of them was a shrinking violet. Hera was, admittedly, most famous as the wife of Zeus who had a famous roving eye; but she fought back and managed to give him a hard time now and again. She once even tied him up with a hundred knots to teach him to behave. Hestia, goddess of the hearth, was certainly domesticated and perhaps the ideal of the middle-aged chauvinist pig with his carpet slippers and cardigan; but Estia could stand up for herself: none of the gods managed to have his way with her and they kept on trying. Even Demeter, goddess of the cornfield, whose priestesses initiated brides and grooms into the secrets of sexual practices, has no husband of her own. Aphrodite is probably the most feminine of the goddesses in the *Playboy* sense; she had a magic girdle which made everybody desire her and had been assigned only one divine duty, to make love. But she is rarely the submissive party. As for the other two, both Athene the goddess of wisdom and Artemis the goddess of hunting would be acceptable on the board of Virago Press. So, in the myths which underpinned Greek culture, women held their own.

There was one myth, recorded by Hesiod, which accounts for the mysterious power of women over men. Prometheus stole fire from Olympus to give to men and, as a punishment, Zeus ordered the creation of woman. She was moulded out of earth as a modest virgin and clothed with an embroidered veil and garlands of spring flowers by the grey-eyed goddess Athene. Then the divine Graces set golden necklaces around her neck and she was called Pandora [all-endowed] because she had been given so many gifts from the gods. She was made irresistible to mortal men and yet she was also given a devious personality, delighting in lies and specious words and sly ways. She was a trap from which there was no escape:

For from her the whole female sex is descended, a great curse to mortal men with whom they live, no help in accursed poverty and ready enough to share wealth. They are like drones which are fed by the bees in their roofed hives and are their partners in crime. For the bees are busy all day till the sun goes down and build white honeycombs while the drones stay at home in the shelter of the hive and fill their bellies with the toil of others. High-thundering Zeus made woman to be a similar curse to mortal men and partner in vexation. But Zeus produced another price to be paid. If a man avoids marriage and all the mischief women cause, and never takes a wife, he comes to his declining years with no-one to look after him in the miseries of old age... [HESIOD, Theogony QUOTED JACT 1984; P95]

The myth explains why it should be that men are never happy with women and yet can't live without them.

The legal evidence certainly suggests that women were oppressed in Athens: they had no vote, could not attend the public Assembly and were barred from holding official jobs. They could not make contracts, which means they could not start a business. For the whole of her life, from birth to death, a female was dependent on a guardian – usually her nearest male blood relative – for legal protection. When she married, he gave the dowry and, worse, if she divorced, he took it back. The position of an heiress was worst of all: she could be claimed in marriage by her nearest male relative, who could even divorce his wife to pick up her fortune. The idea seems to have been that this kept the money in the family. The legal disabilities under which women had to live in Western Europe until the present century had the same object.

If we add to the legal evidence the statements of men about their relations with women, we get, of course, plenty of confirmation that men imagined they were the superior sex. It would be odd if we didn't. The men of Athens were always preening themselves as men will; one of the most quoted statements of the relationship between the sexes is from the speech of a celebrated orator at court:

We have courtesans for our pleasure, concubines for the daily service of our bodies and wives for bearing legitimate children and keeping faithful watch over the goods in our houses. [DEMOSTHENES 59.122]

The speech was made by a man to other men at an all-male gathering. He was being paid for rhetorical flourish and not for careful analysis of social relationships. We might just wonder if he said the same thing when he got home afterwards.

The other much-quoted observation about the position of women is in the Funeral Speech of Pericles, in memory of the Athenians killed in the first year of the Peloponnesian War, where, in giving a direct piece of advice to the women present, he says that women gain great glory by not being talked about by men. This is usually interpreted as meaning simply that women should not be noticed at all, that they should shut themselves away in their houses so that they are not even seen by the public at large, which is a massive put-down from so illustrious a speaker. But he may not have meant anything of the kind; the word used here is that for 'males' and not 'people'. So he may well be saying that the most admirable women are those least talked about when men get together in all-male gatherings. This, given the way the conversation turns on such occasions, is a sentiment we could happily go along with today.

In Sparta the girls were brought up very much as the boys but we don't really know how well women were educated in Athens during the classical age. They needed to be literate, if only to keep the household accounts; Theophrastus, a contemporary of Aristotle, wrote that literacy among women was essential for this purpose. But he went on to say 'Further refinement [i.e. in literacy] makes women too idle in all other spheres, turning them into chatterboxes and busy-bodies' [quoted in Powell 1988; p 342]. The notion, which survived with some vigour into our own age, that advanced education for women was a serious waste of time and money, seems to have been popular amongst prosperous male Athenians. It was the comic poet Menander who pushed the idea into music-hall misogyny: 'Teach a woman letters? A serious mistake! – like giving extra venom to a terrifying snake' [quoted in Powell 1988; p 342].

But if we want to understand the relations between the sexes we can't rely on comedians. There are dumb witnesses from the fifth century which speak volumes. The painted vases often portray domestic scenes; the funerary urns and sculpted tombstones repeatedly show dead wives saying farewell to their husbands and children with a touching dignity. Of one such sculpture, a critic wrote: 'Damasistrate and her husband clasp hands at parting. A child and a kinsman stand beside the chair, but husband and wife have no eyes save for each other, and the calm intensity of their parting gaze answers all questions as to the position of wife and mother in Attic society' [quoted in Kitto 1951; p 228].

And if you feel that this is reading too much into a simple sculpture, listen to the voice of the poet who was at the basis of Greek education and cultural life for centuries, who taught the classical Greeks not only how to write poetry, but how to behave, on the battlefield and at home:

... may the gods grant you your heart's desire; may they give you a husband and a home, and the blessing of harmony that is so much to be desired, since there is nothing better or finer than when two people of one heart and mind keep house as man and wife, a grief to their enemies and a joy to their friends.   [HOMER, Odyssey vi 1991; P 90]

Notable Nudes
(including the partly clad)

c.650	Earliest *kouroi* from Delos
575–550	Calfbearer from Acropolis
540–530	Peplos Kore from Acropolis
470	Bronze Charioteer from Delphi
470–450	Poseidon (or Zeus) striding
460–450	Omphalos Apollo
	Discobolos of Myron
	Marsyas of Myron
450–440	Doryphoros of Polyclitus
447–439	Athena Parthenos of Phidias
442–438	Parthenon friezes
440–430	Diadumenos of Polyclitus
438–431	Pedimental sculptures on Parthenon
435–430	Statue of Zeus at Olympia
350–330	Aphrodite of Cnidos
	Hermes of Olympia

CHAPTER FOUR

Democracy and Drama

If, as for so many recent years seemed likely, the two superpowers had managed to incinerate us all, there would have been a whiff of irony floating over the ashes in the fact that they both did it to defend 'democracy'. The Western powers never stop sounding off about their divine mission to defend it and the Eastern ones are partial to including the word 'democratic' in the names of their republics. The word has been so overused and abused as to have lost all meaning, except, perhaps, to indicate a political system, or aspects of such a system, of which all right-thinking people will approve.

I suppose grown-ups use the word 'democratic' rather as children use the word 'fair': when they feel their rights are threatened or abused or they wish to appeal to a standard of justice which is beyond comment to justify actions which might otherwise be condemned. So animal rights activists exercise their democratic right to blow up biology labs and the popular press defends democracy by publishing in detail what pop stars or royals do in bed.

As everybody knows, 'democracy' means something like 'rule by the people'. It is from two Greek words, *demos*, meaning the commons and *kratos*, meaning power. We all believe we are exercising it when we register our votes. But, apart from the fact that placing a cross on a piece of paper is an act which is almost certainly utterly futile – since no Member of Parliament was ever elected by a majority of one – it would need a lively imagination to connect voting in any direct way with government today. As private citizens, whatever the politicians tell us at election time, we do not enact the legislation which governs our lives, we merely comply with it. And we do not even elect the political party which frames such legislation: every party which has been elected in Britain this century has formed a government in the knowledge that the majority of the electorate did not vote for it.

But in Athens, in the classical age, they not only invented democracy, they practised it. The people did enact the legislation; and they even sacked the leaders they didn't like. Everything was done openly with the public approval of the citizens. It must have been rather like conducting parliamentary debates at the Centre Court, Wimbledon.

The Ecclesia

The popular assembly in Athens and, following her example, after the fifth century almost everywhere, was the Ecclesia, derived from the Greek *eccletos*, meaning 'called out' because they were originally those people called out of their houses by the cry of the herald and assembled in the market place or in a public arena.

In fact, all male citizens over eighteen were entitled to attend – though, as the meetings could take place every eight or ten days, many must have found themselves too busy. But the important principle was that matters of State were conducted, not by professional politicians to the exclusion of public participation as in our own days, but by all citizens. A quorum was probably around five thousand which, given that groups of people always move at the pace of the slowest, must have been sometimes difficult to achieve. There is a scene in a play by Aristophanes of citizens being literally roped in to form a quorum by slaves dragging a rope wet with red paint through the streets: people moved ahead of the rope to avoid being daubed by the paint. This need not mean that they were forced to attend; it could simply be that, as the time to start business approached, stragglers had to be encouraged to get a move on. The painted rope will be fondly thought of by anybody who has ever chaired a public meeting or hosted a dinner party.

The Ecclesia decided on everything: matters of war and peace, on treaties with foreign powers, on legislation and jurisdiction and on taxes and loans, on the granting of citizenship, the death, banishment, or confiscation of property of all citizens and the election of officials.

It was a wide spread of responsibilities and it is something of a mystery how they managed to get anything done at all, since any assembly of five – let alone five thousand – Athenians contains enough diverse opinions to talk away the daylight hours on any subject. And the Ecclesia had to close down at night because then the show of hands by which it voted could not be seen.

So, who spoke there? Well, in theory any adult male Athenian had the right to speak his piece, irrespective of his social class. There was a time when the official question used to be put: 'Who, of those over fifty, wishes to address the Assembly?' but in the fifth and fourth centuries the age qualification was left out and the announcement was simply 'Who wishes to speak to the Assembly?'

Of course there were those who, either from a particular knowledge of a subject, or because they were influential members of society, or simply had the gift of wit or good looks were paid attention. The power to persuade gave political control. The behaviour at the Ecclesia seems to have been generally as squalid as that of the Mother of Parliaments in Westminster and boring or timid speakers were shouted down or hooted at. In Athenian society as elsewhere those born into affluence tended to have an inherited confidence which allowed them to speak with authority – and many of them could afford training in the techniques of public speaking, of which more later. So although there were, in the Ecclesia, no official political parties, there were often minority groups who would organize themselves around an influential speaker and could sway the debate in their own interest. These speakers were known as demagogues, literally 'leaders of the people' and, since the processes of government in Athens were conducted by mass meeting, they had a vital part to play in getting a decision, although Aristophanes already uses the word in the sense we know today, for those who mislead the people by appealing to their baser instincts.

There was a device which restrained this. Its name has survived: it was called ostracism. Any Athenian citizen who felt the city would be better off without somebody could call for a meeting at which anyone could simply write a name on an ostracon, a broken piece of pottery, and if 6000 of them were counted, the individual had to go into exile for ten years. There was no loss of property rights and no particular shame attached to being ostracized. It was simply that the community felt like a rest from someone. If only we had preserved the system today, it would be an effective defence against media personalities and politicians whose faces or opinions we tire of. Not that we have anything against them, just that we need a rest. Ostracism may well have been used in this way in Athens. There's a story of the famous statesman and general Aristides whose name had become proverbial for honest dealing. He was stopped one day by an illiterate Athenian who did not recognize him and asked him to write the name 'Aristides' on an ostracon. When asked why, the man replied simply that he was fed up with hearing Aristides called 'the Just'. Aristides, the story goes, wrote the name.

There is a description of a meeting in the Akharnians, a play by Aristophanes, which, allowing for comic licence, conveys something of the atmosphere. A poor countryman looks on:

Look at this! Plenary session of the Assembly, due to start at sunrise, and not a soul here on the Pnyx! Everybody's down in the market square gossiping, that is when they're not dodging the red rope ... Now me, I'm always the first to get here. So I sit down and, after a bit, when I find out nobody else is coming, I start sighing and yawning and stretching and farting and so on, then I can't think what to do next so perhaps I do some doodling or pick my nose or tot up my debts — but all the time my heart's in the fields out there, and I'm pining for peace. I'm fed up with the city and just craving to get back to my village.

[Lysistrata and other plays 1973; P 50]

The Council of 500 _____

There was a conflict in the organization of government in Athens between the need for the city to have a system which was in daily operation and the desire that all the citizens should take part. A compromise was found in the institution of the Council of 500, which was a sort of steering committee for the Ecclesia, supervising officials and watching over the day-to-day administration. Appointment to the Council was by lot; members had to be over thirty years old; fifty were sent by each of the ten 'tribes' or artificial divisions of the citizen body, to ensure that all the districts were represented. Membership was rotated, members served for terms of one year and no man was allowed to serve more than two terms, which cut down the possibility of corruption. The Council smoothed the work of the Ecclesia by preparing its agenda, the wording of the decrees it could pass and ensuring, on a day-to-day basis, that its decisions were carried out.

Election to the Council conferred prestige and the Athenians were suspicious of those who rose to positions which might undermine the authority of the people. This is why few of the public offices were filled by election – the military officials, naval architects, some of the treasurers and superintendents of the water supply. The rest were chosen by lot on the assumption that any citizen ought to be able to do the jobs available and the lottery prevented power from falling into the hands of those who might feel themselves specially qualified, by talent or experience, to hold office. Perhaps nothing in Athenian democracy is more astonishing to us today than that they should have kept the organization of their lives to such an extent in the hands of the ordinary citizens and away from the experts, the bureaucrats and the politicians.

So Athens was a democracy in the sense that it was run by its citizens. But, as has often been pointed out, the so called democracy of the Greeks, on which our own is meant to have been founded, was the rule of a minority because most of the population of Athens in the great age of democratic rule was not entitled to vote. There were three broad classes of people in Athens: the citizens, the metics, and the slaves.

You could only become a citizen if your father was born one (and, after Pericles' law of 451 your mother too), and you had reached majority which was at the age of eighteen years. There was a provision for the conferring of citizenship rights on a non-citizen and for depriving a citizen of those rights, but these were for special cases. A citizen's apathy about the government of the city was less approved of than it might be today, and the notion that you were too busy making money or searching after truth to vote was frowned on. In fact the idea that individual happiness took precedence over, or could be considered in isolation from the prosperity of, the community — which is unshakeably the foundation of Greek political attitudes today — only came in with the Epicureans after Athens had lost its independence.

The citizens were allowed to devote all this time to politics because they were economically supported by the two other classes of society, the metics and the slaves. Metics were resident aliens, who made up about half the population of Athens. Most of them were Greek, but there were Phrygians, Phoenicians, Egyptians and even Arabs among them. They weren't allowed to vote or to own houses or property and they were liable for a special tax, but it was a very light one, a sum equivalent to only six days work a year for a man and three for a woman. Apart from these restrictions, they were free to prosper: they could own household chattels, including slaves; they were allowed in the public *gymnasia*, from which slaves were excluded; they could celebrate the religious cults of their own country and were allowed to form religious associations, some of which even won converts from among the Athenians. In public services, they occupied the middle ranks and were found as public medical officers or public works contractors; in industry, they were the craftsmen, the weavers, tanners, pottery makers and metal workers; in commerce they were the middlemen, entrepreneurs and bankers. So you could prosper as a metic in Athens, unimpeded by political duties, and earn enough to educate your sons into the professions as artists, doctors, or speechwriters. But, if somebody killed you, you had the discomfort of knowing that, even if he were caught, he would be sent into exile and not executed as he would have been were you an Athenian citizen: your life was not considered as of the same value.

To have been born a metic in Athens had its advantages: to have been born or made into a slave was a disaster. Even the great and humanist philosophers accepted slavery as just. They did this by the argument from human inequality which served slave traders well until the early nineteenth century. Aristotle wrote:

The human race contains certain individuals as inferior to the rest as the body is to the mind or brute beasts are to men. Such persons are destined by nature itself for enslavement, since there is nothing that suits them better than to obey.　　[ARISTOTLE, Politics, 1255a]

Slaves were most commonly acquired through victory in war and, again, Aristotle provides the philosophic justification for this:

Warfare is, in some sense, a legitimate method of acquiring slaves, since it allows for one's need to hunt, not wild beasts only but also men who are born to obey yet refuse to submit to the yoke.　　[IBID; 1256b]

So individuals who were captured in war could be kept as slaves for the rest of their lives unless a ransom was paid, and the populations of whole towns could be enslaved after their capture in war. In peacetime the supply of slaves was kept up by even more morally repulsive methods: they were purchased from surrounding barbarians whose custom it was that the head of the family had the right to sell his children. Within Athens a father who did not wish to rear his child would expose it on a rubbish heap where it died, or could be recovered by someone who would then own it as a slave; the poorest section of the population would occasionally sell themselves into slavery in order to survive; and there was a notorious doctor, Menecrates of Syracuse, who would only treat really desperate cases if the patients signed contracts agreeing to be his slaves if they recovered.

Privately owned slaves were sometimes allowed to marry and breed, not to produce an increase in the stock of free labour – it was cheaper to purchase than to pay for the expense of rearing children – but to encourage loyalty. They could even go through a ceremony which made them members of the household: a newly purchased slave would be seated by the hearth and the mistress of the house would scatter figs and nuts over his head and give him a name as a sign of adoption. Such slaves would share the family prayers, attend family religious festivals and be buried in the family plot. Slaves, in fact, were, for the most part, carefully handled, rather as we might regularly service our washing machines and vacuum cleaners.

Slaves in the public service were the property of the State and carried out a great variety of tasks from public executioner to road sweeper. They could live where they chose, could contract non-legal marriages and have the security of belonging to the ranks, albeit the lowest, of the administrative machine. But, whether public or privately owned, the slave had no legal rights. He did not even exist as a legal person and could not give evidence in court. He was the property of his master and if he tried to run away would be branded with a red-hot iron.

In fifth century Athens, though there were no accurate censuses, there seem to have been around 60 000 to 80 000 slaves in a total population of 250 000, probably about the same proportion as in the American South just before the Civil War.

Whether or not, or how far, Athens could be fairly called a democracy, with its disenfranchised women and social classes, is a question over which academics still argue. A lot depends on the use and definition of terms. The notion of government by the people was recognized and spoken of, the nobility such as the young aristocrat Alcibiades calling it a 'generally acknowledged folly'. Attempts were made by the Council of 500, on to which, by a whole series of stratagems, the better-off seemed to land themselves, to impose a form of guidance which constituted political control, but they were never wholly successful. The Ecclesia met less frequently, and its votes were rarely counted, decisions being on a general show of hands. It was swayed by emotional oratory as much as rational argument and there is some evidence that, at the height of democracy in Athens, the poorer classes still seem to have 'loved a Lord': Alcibiades was given a high office of state because his team of horses had won at the Olympic games.

But far more important than the question of voting was the concept of isonomia, or equality before the law. This protected the poorer classes for a century against the oppression of the well-to-do. It was an ideal which had not occurred to any previous society and which was, in practice, rejected by most subsequent ones. The greatness of Athens lies in her having conceived and, for a time, nurtured such an ideal.

Athenian democracy was based on the right of her citizens to express themselves in public. The most magnificent and lasting testimonial to this is Greek theatre.

Drama

The main barrier between ourselves and Greek drama is that we approach it with the wrong expectations. To us, drama is something which is going on around us most of the time and we can take it or leave it by switching on the television or going out to the theatre or a cinema. Greek audiences did not amble down to the theatre one evening because they happened to feel like taking in a play. Theatre was not something readily available on a take it or leave it basis, a casual way of distracting yourself or having your fancy tickled.

Greek plays were put on as part of the celebrations for the god Dionysus which were held in January and March. At the spring festival in Athens, the whole population as well as hundreds of strangers who turned up for the occasion would throng the theatre on a number of successive days and be part of a majestic civic ceremony.

The performances were paid for as public works by wealthy citizens who would be assigned the honour of footing the bill for the scenery and costumes as well as paying for the training of the musicians and the chorus. Even writing plays, in classical Greece, was a competitive activity. At the comic festivals, five single plays by five different playwrights would be put on in competition with each other.

At the tragic festivals three playwrights would each enter four plays: a tragic trilogy followed by a lighter 'satyr' play. There was fierce competition because the prize, although it was only a plain ivy wreath, carried with it great public honour.

Come to think of it, there is pretty fierce competition between our television networks today and the prize is commercial success, which we are rather keener on than public honour, but the effects of the competition on standards are rather different. This may be because the prizes for Greek drama were awarded by a panel of ten judges and not on public acclaim. Had they been given on a show of hands after the performance, the quality of Greek plays might have been very different.

Tragedy

The first and most obvious objection to our being moved by classical Greek tragedies is that they don't deal with real people. We have come to expect that plays and films are about recognizable human situations and so move us to laughter or tears because we can see the possibility of being involved in those situations ourselves. The most massively successful dramatic productions of our time – if you judge success by the number of people who watch them – are our television soap operas. They are popular because they stick close to real life and its problems. We recognize in them the people we see in the streets and on the buses.

So how are we to cope with plays that deal with mythical larger-than-life characters whose actions are controlled by the gods and who, under their influence, get up to such *outré* activities as murdering their fathers, going to bed with their mothers, or sacrificing their daughters to improve the weather? Surely such characters are so remote from us, not only in time but in psychology, that we can no more respond to their anxieties than weep at the frustrations of the Daleks.

There is a clue in an interview I heard with an actress who had achieved regular employment, a rare luxury in the profession, and the bonuses of a comfortable life-style and national fame as a character in a television series. Asked the stock question about unfulfilled ambitions, she admitted that hardly a week went by when she didn't long to play

Lady Macbeth. She wasn't by nature given to arranging for her husband to stab their house-guests or to enjoying bouts of insanity; she just longed to be extended beyond doing the housework and coping with teenage tantrums.

It is in this capacity to extend us that Greek tragedy scores. Because our most basic emotions, our fundamental moral character, tend to be unexercised by the daily business of living: they are more likely to be shaped by the books we read, the plays and films we see than by the people we meet. And the Greeks knew how to use the myths which treat of the most basic of human emotions and moral perceptions in a way which transcends the particular situation of a dramatic plot and makes the audience feel their living truth. We are all limited in our freedom by the capacity to hurt other people. And the classic situation in Greek tragedy, where a character has to choose between two alternatives, either of which has painful consequences, is close to our lives.

Bernard Williams who, as Professor of Moral Philosophy at Oxford University, has, as we shall see, a high opinion of the Greek contribution to his subject, quotes with enthusiasm a remark of Nietzsche that one of the great glories of the Greeks is that they didn't put their best into reflection. He meant by this that the most powerful things the Greeks have to teach us about moral life are not to be learned from their philosophy. Tragedy presents these things in an unmediated and compelling way which brings them home far more powerfully than philosophical dialogue. So you can't have a sense of the Greek experience, even at the level of moral ideas, just from the philosophers; you get that only from the epics and the tragedies.

The Greek tragedians, even when they deal with ancient myths, are, paradoxically, closer to us and our view of the world than are the philosophers who challenged those myths. Because the great philosophers all wrote as if there was a rational order in the world and if only we could organize our thinking processes properly we could get in tune with that order. Aristotle thought that the world was at the centre of the Universe and that human rationality had a special relationship to divine rationality. And if you take the great belief systems that came later, they still hold that humans have a special place in the Universe: either God, the Creator, sent his only son to save them, or made laws which the prophets could mediate to us as in Judaism and Islam. Later, Marxism taught a large percentage of the world's population that the order of history was such that, in the end, Man could free himself by his own efforts.

The Greeks didn't believe anything like that: we could behave honourably but, on the whole, the Universe wasn't interested in us. It certainly wasn't on our side. Lots of human efforts were doomed to failure, not for great epic reasons but through sheer bad luck. So human values, the Greeks saw, were contingent, limited, and dependent on love and fame.

Now it probably seems to the majority of people today that the Greek view of life comes closer to bearing out their actual experience of it than any of the great systems of belief, religious or other. In fact, we're probably closer to the Greeks today than any age which existed between them and us, because most ages in between believed in a cosmological order which affirms human purposes and makes sense of them outside themselves. The Greeks didn't. And, by and large, we don't.

There is, though, a necessary condition for getting on with Greek tragedy. It's one which usually, I've noticed, makes classics masters turn slightly pink and start shuffling their feet, because the occupational hazard of teaching classics is to be thought out of date and slightly pompous. And however you try to express this condition, you run the risk of being labelled both. The condition is that you be prepared to take seriously notions of duty, honour, justice; possibly even – dare one say it – eternal verities. They may not have a daily relevance in our lives but you have to think they matter. If you've managed to take to heart and live by the splendid pragmatism of the teaching that 'nothing matters very much and few things matter at all', then the next bit is not for you. Move on to Comedy.

Those of us who are less certain about the ultimates can turn to the Greek tragedians with a reasonable expectation that they have something to say to us. There is, of course, a problem in coming across them on the printed page: they didn't after all write to be read. Drama is from a Greek word which means 'doing' and it necessarily involves action. So that reading about the Greek tragedians who have made so great an impact on world literature might seem a bit like reading musical criticism: if you haven't experienced the performance you may be missing the essential. But on the other hand we have to admit that nobody really knows how the plays were performed, what was the part of the chorus and of the music, both of which must have made these works have an impact closer to Grand Opera than Agatha Christie. There have been many attempts to recreate the authentic atmosphere of the Greek theatre down the years but those of us who have missed out on them can take some comfort in the words of Peter Levi in his *History of Greek Literature*: 'All modern attempts to recreate the ancient tragic conventions in the theatre have failed more or less disastrously'. [p 153]

Aeschylus

Aeschylus was the father of Greek, and hence of world, drama. He found it as a performance in which a chorus danced around the stage while an actor recited a story, and hit on the idea of having a second actor on the stage so that dialogue could take place. At least he is commonly credited with the idea. Scholars have disputed this, as they have discounted the story that he was killed when a passing eagle, mistaking his shining bald head for a rock, dropped a tortoise on it.

It is difficult to overestimate Aeschylus. He not only invented the art of tragedy but also took it to heights which have never been surpassed. Even his contemporaries knew how good he was and, on his death, the Athens Assembly made a decree that any citizen who revived one of his plays should be supported by a chorus at public expense, which allowed him to go on winning prizes in the dramatic competitions against living authors. Aeschylus deals with the great human issues – Victor Hugo compared him to an Old Testament prophet – but he does so with a simple directness that makes your hair stand on end. 'If Aeschylus does not leave you excited and transfigured,' wrote H. D. F. Kitto in the most readable little book ever written about the Greeks, 'you have not been getting Aeschylus' [Kitto 1951; p 250].

The tragedy of human existence as depicted by Aeschylus is that man is in the grip of half-understood forces which bring him into situations in which he must undergo and cause pain. He sees around him good people suffering and the wicked in prosperity; he has no notion of a compensatory hell and heaven in the afterlife; the distribution of happiness and misery is in the hands of blind fate and not of blind justice. In these basic observations and beliefs he is our contemporary.

Aeschylus wrote more than seventy plays, of which only seven, possibly six (the scholars are still arguing about the *Prometheus*) have survived. But we do have the complete trilogy of the *Oresteia*, which Algernon Swinburne described as 'the greatest achievement of the human mind' so it's surely worth giving it a try. The first play of the trilogy, the *Agamemnon*, is only as long as the first two acts of *Hamlet*, so the effort of making contact with the mind of Aeschylus is a small one. Here is something of the flavour of it.

The play opens at night in the tenth year of the Trojan war — the year in which a prophecy has said that Troy will fall. A watchman on a high roof of Agamemnon's palace is waiting for the signal fire that will announce the fall of Troy and fighting off sleep by watching the stars:

I know them all, and watch them
Setting and rising; but the one light I long to see
Is a new star, the promised sign, the beacon flare
To speak from Troy and utter one word, 'Victory!'   [AESCHYLUS 1959; P41]

Suddenly a beacon flames from a mountain top to the east and he shouts and dances for joy. Troy has fallen. The long wait is over. But he breaks off in the middle of the dance and we sense a shadow fall. He won't explain:

Well, I speak to those
Who understand me; to the rest — my door is shut.   [IBID; P42]

The mood of the play is set and this contrast between light and darkness, hope and fear, is to remain in tension through the play.

We begin to learn of a dark menace from the past as the chorus tells how the Greek fleet, setting out for Troy, was suddenly struck by head winds from the North. Agamemnon, leader of the alliance, had offended the goddess Artemis who could only be appeased by the sacrifice of his daughter. He had to make the tragic decision between his duty as commander of the fleet and his duty as a father:

Disband the fleet, sail home, and earn
The deserter's badge — abandon my command,
Betray the alliance — now? The wind must turn,
There must be sacrifice, a maid must bleed —   [IBID; P 49]

He chose to sacrifice Iphigeneia and the fleet went on to victory. But the mother of Iphigeneia, his wife Clytaemnestra, has waited ten years to face her husband, the murderer of her child.

She appears and hails the victory and tells the crowd that she is preparing the best welcome for her lord. May he find her as true and faithful as on the day he left:

... in all ways unchanged.
No seal of his have I unsealed in these ten years.
Of pleasure bound with other men, or any breath
Of scandal I know no more than how to dip hot steel.   [IBID; P 64]

She claims to be faithful but the chorus — and we — know that she lies. She has taken another lord into the palace. Tension and irony again.

When Agamemnon appears she greets him as a returning hero and tells of the despair she felt in the long years without him. Her anguish drove her to the point of suicide:

These fears explain
Why our child is not here to give you fitting welcome,

She leaves the name of the child unspoken and we feel she may be about to confront him with the sacrifice of Iphigeneia, but she pauses and goes on:

Our true love's pledge, Orestes. Have no uneasiness.
He is in Phocis, a guest of Strophius, your well tried friend   [IBID; P 72]

The confrontation has been postponed.

The moment of crisis passes but the anticipation builds. She goes on to explain that their son Orestes has been sent away to be raised in another city in case of an uprising at home. We know that she is living with another man and there is another explanation for the exile of her son. So whenever Clytaemnestra speaks we have come to sense a double meaning in her words. But she protests her suffering and loyalty to Agamemnon:

... my sleepless eyes are sore
With weeping by the lamp long lit for you in vain.
In dreams, the tenuous tremours of the droning gnat
Roused me from dreadful visions of more deaths for you
Than could be compassed in the hour that slept with me.   [IBID; P 73]

And then comes the beginning of a dramatic and theatrical ritual. The women enter carrying crimson tapestries which they spread on the ground between the king and the doors of the palace. Clytaemnestra invites him to tread on them:

Now, dearest husband, come, step from your chariot.
But do not set to earth, my lord, the conquering foot
That trod down Troy.   [IBID; P 73]

Is she testing him? When men overreach themselves, the gods strike them down. The primal sin is that of self-assertion, of acting like a god. He knows this and protests – only the gods deserve the pomps of honour and spread tapestries, men should walk on the earth. But she tempts him: if Priam of Troy had won, he would have accepted the display, as Agamemnon is the great victor, he could give way to her in this little matter and finally, if he willingly surrenders to his wife he remains the victor. So Agamemnon, tempted to do what he knows is wrong, agrees and hopes only that by removing his boots he can avert the anger of the gods.

As he strides to the palace, Clytaemnestra emphasizes the sacrilege by hailing him as the greatest of the gods:

Zeus! Zeus! Fulfiller! Now fulfil these prayers of mine;
And let thy care accomplish all that is thy will!.   [IBID; P96]

The old men huddle in terror at the doors and they – and we – expect to hear the shriek of the dying Agamemnon. But Aeschylus delays the crisis and increases the tension further by bringing forward Cassandra, daughter of the king of Troy, who has been brought back as a prize by Agamemnon and has been watching everything. She has been given the gift of prophecy but is also fated to be disbelieved whenever she prophesies. Now she adds to the mounting horror of the situation by seeing visions of the Furies, smelling the freshly spilt blood and shrieking in terror. Finally she goes knowingly to her death through the palace doors. Her last words are calm:

Alas for human destiny! Man's happiest hours
Are pictures drawn in shadow. Then ill fortune comes,
And with two strokes the wet sponge wipes the drawing out.
And grief itself's hardly more pitiable than joy.   [IBID; P88]

We hear the death cries of Agamemnon – the convention was that violence took place off stage – and then the doors are opened to reveal his body lying with that of Cassandra, and Clytaemnestra, sword in hand, standing over them. She tells of the killing in vivid detail:

So falling he belched forth his life; with cough and retch
There spurted from him bloody foam in a fierce jet,
And spreading, spattered me with drops of crimson rain;
While I exulted...   [IBID; P91]

Aegisthus, her lover, enters with his bodyguard and stands in triumph over Agamemnon's body. Only the crowd of old men are horrified and raise their sticks to threaten the usurper and the murdering queen:

Chorus:	You'll find no Argive grovel at a blackguard's feet.
Aegisthus:	Enough! Some day later I'll settle scores with you.
Chorus:	Not if Fate sets Orestes on the Argos road.
Aegisthmus:	For men in exile, hopes are meat and drink; I know.
Chorus:	Rule on, grow fat defiling Justice — while you can.
Aegisthus:	You are a fool; in time you'll pay me for those words.
Chorus:	Brag blindly on — a cock that struts before his hen!
Clytemnaestra:	Pay no heed to this currish howling. You and I,
	Joint rulers will enforce due reverence for our throne.

[IBID; P 100]

The play ends with the mention of the name of Orestes and the reminder to the audience that he is now a grown man, in exile, and that Fate, as they know will set him on the Argos road to avenge his father. The joint rulers have but a little time; the sequel has been signalled.

Sophocles

Although Aeschylus wrote the sequel, so did many other dramatists, among them Sophocles, and it may be interesting to take up the story here with his version of it. Sophocles was a boy actor who, by the time he was twenty-eight, was acting in his own plays. He wrote 123 of them but only seven have survived. He had a very successful career, winning the prize twenty-four times, and managed to fit in time to be treasurer of the Athenian empire and twice a general in the Athenian army as well. As a dramatist, he is less sonorous, less apocalyptic than Aeschylus and his characters, as we shall see, are perhaps touched with more humanity.

His *Electra* opens with Orestes standing outside the palace of Aegisthus and Clytaemnestra, plotting how to get in and avenge his father without arousing suspicion. He decides to send in his aged tutor with the news that he has been killed in a chariot race so they will be off their guard; he will then announce himself as bearing the ashes in an urn. This will gain him entrance. The scene changes and his sister

Electra enters at once mourning hopelessly the death of her father and shouting defiance at her mother and Aegisthus for living in luxury on the throne and sharing the bed of the man they murdered. Her sister Chrysothemis tries to persuade her to be reconciled to her fate since they are both powerless. Electra, she says, is making her own life worse by protesting and risking banishment. But Electra says she would welcome it:

Chrysothemis: *Are you out of your mind? Can you want to suffer so?*
Electra: *Yes to escape, far, far out of the sight of all of you.*
Chrysothemis: *With no regret for life as you know it now?*
Electra *Life as I know it! How wonderful!*
Chrysothemis: *It could be, if you chose to make it so.*
Electra: *You mean if I betrayed my best-beloved?*
Chrysothemis: *Nothing of the sort; only obey your masters.*
Electra: *And cringe, as you do? I couldn't find it in me.*
Chrysothemis: *No-one would wish you to fall by your own folly.*
Electra: *I will fall, if need be, for my father's sake.*
Chrysothemis: *But I believe our father will pardon us.*
Electra: *Cowards believe such comfortable things.* [SOPHOCLES 1953; P 80]

The discussion is already a believable interchange between two human characters, sisters with different points of view and not the personifications of high moral principles.

Chrysothemis brings offerings from Clytaemnestra for the grave of Agamemnon but Electra persuades her not to place them there:

How can you think the dead
Could gratefully take such tributes from the fiend
That mercilessly killed and butchered him
And wiped her bloody sword upon his hair?
Will these gifts clean her hands? Never on earth.
Throw them away.
This is what you must give him . . .
A lock of your own bright hair . . . and this of mine —
In my poor state it's all I have to give —

> There ... it's not glossy like yours ... This girdle too,
> It's only plain, but take it.   [IBID; P 82]

Her situation is moving but the audience knows that Orestes is already nearby. And the chorus senses it:

> The Avenger lies in wait; the feet, the hands
> Are closing in, the bronze hoof stamps   [IBID; P 83]

In the next scene, Clytaemnestra gives a reasoned statement of the motive for her killing Agamemnon:

> This father of yours, whom you never stop weeping for, did a thing no other Greek had dared to do, when he so ruthlessly sacrificed your sister to the gods — the child whom he had begotten, at little cost of course compared to mine who bore her. No doubt you can tell me why he did this, and for whose sake? For the Greeks, maybe? And who gave them the right to take my daughter's life?   [IBID; P 84]

Electra then puts the case for her father, saying that he had thoughtlessly killed a stag sacred to Artemis and that the goddess therefore demanded this price of him before she would let the fleet sail for Troy. So he was forced, against his will, to make the sacrifice of his daughter. And if Clytaemnestra wants to live by the code of a life for a life, then she, of course, must be killed to pay for her husband.

When the tutor arrives with the false report of the death of Orestes, he describes the accident with such vigour and colourful detail that Clytaemnestra is convinced and is delighted. Electra is grief-stricken and pours out her heart to the stranger who arrives with the urn containing the ashes of her brother. But the stranger is Orestes: he reveals himself and explains his plan to murder their mother:

> **Orestes:**   And remember, you must not let your mother see
>   A smile upon your face, when we go in;
>   Be weeping still, for my pretended death.
>   When we have won, there will be time to smile
>   And rejoice to your heart's content.
> **Electra:**   Dear, I will do everything you ask me;
>   You are the cause of all my happiness,
>   I would not hinder you for all the world.   [IBID; P 109]

When Orestes enters the house and the cries of their mother are heard through the closed doors, Electra shouts to him to strike and strike again. When Aegisthus arrives the body of Clytaemnestra lies covered next to the opened palace doors. He thinks it is Orestes and uncovers it in delight. Only when he has seen the dead face of his queen does Orestes thrust him through the doors to his death. The chorus proclaims that freedom has been won for the House of Atreus and the play ends.

Euripides

The angry young man of Greek tragedy, Euripides, was never quite such a success in his lifetime as Aeschylus and Sophocles. Although he wrote ninety-two plays, he only managed to win four prizes and this could be because his approach was different and unpopular. Tragedy had concerned itself with the great issues of human passions in conflict with divine purpose. Aeschylus had done this by drawing superhuman characters who speak in echoing poetry, Sophocles had added touches of humanity, writing, as Aristotle put it, characters who are 'like ourselves, only nobler', intelligent people trying to come to grips with the dark forces that seem to sway their destinies. Euripides brought them down to earth and wrote of human tragedy caused by human frailty. This is not to say his characters are commonplace – you wouldn't run across Medea or Electra on the bus or the tube – but when they wrestle with the mystery of evil it is as a force within themselves and not a compulsion sent from the gods. In this, at least, they are our contemporaries.

Euripides also wrote an Electra and if we compare it with the play of Sophocles we shall feel the contrast. The comparison will also help us understand how it was possible for so many plays to be watchable when written on so few story lines – and it has the advantage that we don't have to learn yet another set of names and relationships.

When the play opens, Electra has been married off to a local peasant. Aegisthus has arranged this in the hope that work on the land and bringing up a string of children will take her mind off revenge. It hasn't worked. The peasant respects her royal person and she is still a virgin. He also tries to stop her from doing farm work as she 'was not made for toil' so she has the time to wander about moaning:

My nights are drawn out with tears,
My hopeless days are occupied with tears.
Look at me — my hair uncared for,
My dress in tatters!
Would not his daughter's appearance
Bring shame to King Agamemnon...?   [EURIPIDES 1963; P 11]

She weeps continually for her murdered father and also for her own squalor which turns out to be self-imposed since the local women offer her clothes and a gold necklace to attend a celebration. She turns them down with a cry of self-pity:

Mourn for the king who died,
Mourn for the prince who lives
Exile and outcast in a foreign country...
While I, banished from my ancestral palace
Live in a labourer's cottage,
Eating out my heart among these bleak crags.   [IBID; P 111]

As for the prince who lives outcast in the foreign country, when Orestes does turn up, he does not dare enter Argos until he has found out what his sister feels about the situation. He meets Electra and says he is a friend of Orestes. She gives him a message for her brother:

First how I'm dressed; how I'm stabled here; the filth
That weighs me down, the squalid shack that has replaced
My royal palace; how I must sit at the loom and weave
Cloth for my own dress, or go naked; never a feast
On holy days, never a dance; I cannot mix
With wives, myself a virgin; as for Castor, who,
Before he joined the gods was courting me, his cousin,
How can I think of him?   [IBID; P 115]

The only hope she has is that Orestes will return one day to avenge her wrongs and his father's death. This is obviously the time when Orestes should reveal himself and the theatre echo to shrieks of delight. But Euripides has drawn a complex character. His Orestes is unsure of himself and needs to know what will be expected of him. So he asks:

Orestes: *Suppose Orestes comes, how will he deal with this?*
Electra: *You ask that? You insult him. Is the time not ripe?*
Orestes: *But, once he came, how could he carry out this killing?*
Electra: *Let him be resolute, as his father's murderers were.*
Orestes: *Would you be resolute and help him kill your mother?*
Electra: *I would — with the same axe by which my father died.*
Orestes: *I'll tell him, then, that you are steadfast?*
Electra: *When I have shed Her blood to requite his, then I can die content.*
Orestes: *I wish Orestes could be by, to hear you speak.*   [IBID; P 114]

He won't reveal himself because he knows that his sister will never let him off the hook if he does. And he lacks the boldness and resolution of the superhuman hero. He is vacillating and fallible. Eventually he is recognized by an old man and has to go ahead with the murders. That of Aegisthus is shabby and demeaning. Orestes finds him peacefully preparing for a festival, 'in a well-watered plot, cutting young myrtle leaves to make a garland for his head'. Aegisthus invites him in to share the feast and, when Orestes offers to skin the sacrificial bull, hands him the knife. As the king bends over the carcase:

Orestes rose on his toes, and struck him on the joint of the neck,
Shattering his spine. His whole body, from head to foot
Writhed, shuddered in death agony.   [IBID; P 134]

Electra, meanwhile, has sent a message to her mother that she has just been delivered of her first child, in the knowledge that Clytaemnestra would visit her. When she arrives, she is conciliatory. She explains that even though Agamemnon had wrongly sacrificed their daughter simply to go to Troy and bring back Helen — a randy wife who had run away — she would not have turned savage and killed him if he had not brought home Cassandra, the mad prophetess, to be his second wife. Two women in one house was impossible to bear and, in her passion, she killed him. She still regrets what she has done.

Electra replies that it is too late for regrets but asks if her mother will do her the favour of making the necessary sacrifice for the firstborn son. Clytaemnestra goes into the house to do this and is killed by her children.

When they come out to speak of what they have done, Euripides spares no detail to show the murder as squalid and despicable:

Orestes: Did you see how, in her agony,
    She opened her gown, thrust forth her breast,
    And showed it to me as I struck?
    Her body that gave me birth
    Sprawled there on the ground.
    I had her by the hair . . .

Chorus: I know what torture you went through;
    I heard her shriek — your own mother.

Electra: Yes; as she uttered that shriek
    She was putting her hand on my face;
    'My child, I implore you', she said.
    Then she hung around my neck
    So that the sword fell out of my hand.

Chorus: Wretched, miserable woman! How could you bear
    To see with your own eyes
    Your mother gasping out her life?

Orestes: I held my cloak over my eyes,
    While with my sword I performed sacrifice,
    Driving the blade into my mother's throat.   [IBID; P 147]

There is no sense here of characters who carry out the commands of a higher power, of humans bending their wills to conform with divine decrees, just a couple of fallible people driven to a terrible deed by the evil that exists within themselves.

There were quite possibly more Greek dramas staged in the world in 1992 than during any year since ancient times, according to Oliver Taplin, Fellow and Tutor in Classics at Magdalene College, Oxford. They were performed by professional and amateur companies, not only in Europe, but in Japan and South America, which seems to indicate that theatre people are finding something in Greek tragedy they don't get elsewhere. And something of what they find has to be universal because of the success with which it is performed in so many different countries.

These plays bring their audience face to face with terrifying possibilities that are still open. And the way in which Greek tragedy is performed makes it possible to face those terrors. The ritual, the ceremonial, the formality, the chorus, the poetry all contribute to put us in a frame of mind which is different from that in which we face our everyday experience.

Where we are confronted by violence in the television news we react by distancing ourselves from the experiences to which we cannot afford to react fully as humans. So the experience of encountering actual human suffering as directly presented to us by television cameras is a dehumanizing one because if we reacted with the appropriate human feelings of horror or sympathy we should be disabled from going about our normal lives. But Greek tragedy is presented in a formal way which allows us to be open to its emotions without switching off our sensibilities. Under the special controlled circumstances of Greek tragedy which the audience accepts have been set aside for experiencing terrors and facing up to choices, people are enabled to engage directly with what is portrayed. So the poetry and the pathos of Greek tragedy can affect us far more deeply than the harsh realities of the real world and we may be moulded more by theatre than by current affairs.

Comedy

Comic writers got their laughs two and a half thousand years ago by using the same material as they draw on today: what we have to put up with from the government, our wives/husbands, intellectuals and the literary crowd, bodily functions, especially excretion and sex.

Nobody wrote both tragedy and comedy. No actors played both. Comedy grew up alongside tragedy, almost as a competitor to it and in many ways its opposite. Tragedy is set in the great days of the heroic past, comedy in the everyday present, its characters having the names of contemporary citizens. And yet it was fantastic. You could say and do anything. There were hardly any restraints and in the carnival atmosphere anything went. Tragedy was decorous and noble, comedy its opposite.

Aristophanes

We know almost nothing about the most famous writer of Greek comedy apart from what we can gather from his writing and his appearance as a character in Plato's *Symposium*. As Plato was a personal friend of Aristophanes, it's likely that the portrait is true to life, and the first thing we learn about him is that he has a hangover from a party the previous night. Socrates makes the comment that Aristophanes is well briefed to make a speech in praise of love, since his 'entire business lies with Dionysus and Aphrodite', which could mean either that he was preoccupied with drinking and sex in his private life or that his profession was to serve these divinities – or both.

He certainly made good use of their potentiality for laughs. There is no funnier scene in the whole of theatrical history than that in Lysistrata between Cinesias and Myrrhine. The situation is that the women have all taken an oath to deprive the men of sex until they stop fighting each other. This deprivation has left Cinesias with a permanent and painful erection and he brings it to the Acropolis, where the women have congregated, in search of relief from his wife. He even carries their baby and slaps it when he gets within earshot so she will pay attention to its cries. She comes out:

Cinesias: *But won't you let me make love to you? It's been such a long time!*
Myrrhine: *No. Mind you, I'm not saying I don't love you . . .*
Cinesias: *You do, Myrrie love? Why won't you let me, then?*
Myrrhine: *What, you idiot, in front of the baby?*
Cinesias: *No – er – Manes, take it home.* [The slave departs with the baby] *All right, darling, it's out of the way, let's get on with it.*

Myrrhine:	*Don't be silly, there's nowhere we can do it here.*
Cinesias:	*What's wrong with Pan's grotto?*
Myrrhine:	*And how am I supposed to purify myself before going back into the Acropolis? It's sacred ground, you know.*
Cinesias:	*Why, there's a perfectly good spring next to it.*
Myrrhine:	*You're not asking me to break my oath!*
Cinesias:	*On my own head be it. Don't worry about that, darling.*
Myrrhine:	*All right, I'll go and get a camp bed.*
Cinesias:	*Why not on the ground?*
Myrrhine:	*By Apollo — I love you very much but not on the ground.* [She goes into the Acropolis]
Cinesias:	*Well, at least she does love me, that I can be sure of.*
Myrrhine:	[returning with a bare camp bed] Here you are. You must lie down while I take off my — Blast it! We need a — what do you call it? — a mattress. [ARISTOPHANES 1973; P 218]

And so the scene goes on, Myrrhine just on the point of submitting and then remembering something else she must have first and Cinesias rolling about in priapic agony while she dashes off to get a pillow for herself, a pillow for him, a blanket for them both, a jar of ointment which turns out to be the wrong one so she goes off to fetch another and, eventually, of course, runs off and slams the gates.

The comic possibilities of sexual frustration have been exploited by playwrights down the centuries but Aristophanes did it first and he did it best.

We are often told that we miss out on much of the humour in Aristophanes because it depends on verbal puns which don't often translate or on references to political situations which, without an intimate knowledge of the politics of his time, we can't understand. But political situations repeat themselves and there is surely something about his play *The Assembly Women* that rings bells for us today.

The play opens just before dawn in an Athens street. A woman is stealthily letting herself out of her house, anxious not to waken her husband and carrying his cloak and staff. Other women appear with their husband's clothes and some apologize for being late:

I haven't slept a wink. That man of mine! He comes from Salamis, do I need to say more?
He's been at me all night, I wonder the bedclothes aren't torn to shreds. I've only just
managed to pinch his cloak. [ARISTOPHANES 1988; p 223]

They have all brought false beards and it turns out that they are
heading for the Assembly where, dressed as men, they are going to
pass a law handing over the government of the city to women. The
men have made such a mess of things the city needs female insight,
common sense and administrative ability to get things in order again.

They put on their home-made beards and try out a few prepared
speeches but don't seem quite to have got the hang of things and
keep swearing by the goddesses instead of by the gods. One of them
asks their leader, Praxagora, how on earth frail women can hope to
sway the Assembly:

Praxagora: *Nothing easier, I should think. It's well known that the most successful young*
orators are the ones who get laid most often. So we start off with certain
natural advantages   [IBID; p 226]

But, when she comes to make her speech, it turns out she has no
need of such advantages. She is powerfully persuasive. She condemns
the way the citizens of Athens line their own pockets without a
thought for the State and proposes that the government be handed
over to the women: 'They are, after all, the people to whom we look
for the efficient management of our homes.' She goes on to say that
the men create problems because they can't resist fiddling about with
institutions that are working perfectly well, whereas women know a
good thing when they see it and will preserve it:

They bake cakes, as they've always done. They infuriate their husbands, as they've always
done. They conceal lovers in the house, as they've always done. They buy themselves little
extras on the side, as they've always done. They drink their wine neat, as they've always
done. They enjoy a bit of sex, as they've always done. And so, gentlemen, let us waste no
time in fruitless debate or in asking what they propose to do, but quite simply hand over the
reins of government to them, and let them get on with the job. In doing so we need only
remind ourselves, firstly that, as mothers, they will naturally be concerned for the safety of
our soldiers; and who is more likely than a mother to ensure them an adequate supply of

food? Further that a woman is a highly resourceful creature when it comes to ways of raising money; and, certainly, when in office she will never allow herself to be taken in — she knows all the tricks already. [IBID; P230]

That the art of politics is simply an extension of good housekeeping with the corollary that women are best at it is a sentiment which has a topical ring, in no country more than Britain today.

But the play is not a serious political comment, it is closer to farce or pantomime, and the next scene has Praxagora's husband emerging from the house in urgent need of a bowel movement. Because she has taken his cloak and shoes, he is dressed in her yellow dress and Persian slippers, in which regalia he squats by the side of the street. He hopes to get away unseen but it turns out he is constipated and his neighbours appear before he is finished, all complaining that their clothes have been stolen. Then a citizen comes from the Assembly to report that a strange lot of very pale men — 'we thought they must be shoemakers, they looked so pale' — had filled the Assembly and that the vote had been taken to hand over the government to the women.

At this point Praxagora declares her policy:

Praxagora: ... *first of all, I shall declare all land, all money, and all private possessions to be common property. And from this common stock it shall be our job — the women's job — to feed you and manage your affairs sensibly and economically.*

Chremes: *What about the people who don't own any land, but have all their wealth hidden away in silver or in Persian gold?*

Praxagora: *They must put it all into the common pool and not try to hold onto it by committing perjury.*

Blepyrus: *Which is how they got it in the first place.*

Praxagora: *But now it won't be useful to them in any case.*

Chremes: *How do you make that out?*

Praxagora: *No one will be motivated by need: everybody will have everything — loaves, cutlets, cakes, warm cloaks, wine, head wreaths, chickpeas. So what advantage will there be in hanging on to one's wealth? If you can think of any, it's more than I can.* [IBID; P 242]

Her husband thinks up a reason for keeping back a store of private wealth so that a man can pay for the services of a young woman. He is told that the services will be given free because all women will be available to all men. The obvious objection to this arrangement is that the prettiest ones will be in demand and the ugly ones left out, so the proposal is that, if a man wants to sleep with a pretty girl, he must first make love to an ugly one. Aristophanes does not pass by the comic possibilities of this situation.

A young man serenades a young girl passionately and knocks at her door. But another door opens and an old hag appears:

Old hag: *Yes, what is it? Oh, are you looking for me?*

Young man: *Far from it.*

Old hag: *Oh you must be. You were battering on my door.*

Young man: *I'm damned if I was.*

Old hag: *What do you want, then, coming here with a torch?*

Young man: *I'm looking for a man with a limp.*

Old hag: *With a limp what?*

Young man: *He wouldn't do for you. You won't get what you're waiting for.*

Old hag: *I will, by Aphrodite, whether you like it or not.*

Young man: *I'm sorry, madam, we're not dealing with any cases more than sixty years old; we've put those off till later. Just now we're polishing off the under twenties.*

Old hag: *That was under the old rules, sweetheart. Now you have to take us first. That's the law.*

Young man: *It's optional: 'No player obliged to take a piece unless he wishes to do so.'...*

Old hag: *It's the law that says you must come with me.*

Young man: *Read me what it says.*

Old hag: *I was just going to. 'Be it known that the women hereby enact as follows: if a young man desire a young woman, it shall not be lawful for him to screw the same unless and until he has pleasured an old one; and if he refuses so to pleasure her in due priority it shall be lawful for the older woman to seize him by the tool and drag him away forthwith.'*

Young man: *Yow! I'm in for a long-drawn-out evening, I can see that.*

[IBID; PP 256-7]

We tend to wish upon all comic writers a mission to reform because, by holding up particular personalities or institutions to ridicule, they encourage contempt for them and the awareness of the need for change. And it's very tempting to look behind the laughter and try to get at the cast of mind that led the writer to select his targets. Aristophanes has not lacked interpreters who have divided and classified his plays neatly into periods reflecting different political attitudes; but this is contentious stuff because, although he satirized prominent men and popular movements, he didn't exempt anybody or any class. If he found a personality, a situation, a popular trend in thought or behaviour could make an audience laugh, he used it. His greatness lies in this universality and the fact that his audiences are still laughing today.

Drama from the classical period

Aeschylus   525–456

Persians	472
Seven against Thebes	467
Suppliants	463
Agamemnon	
Libation Bearers (Oresteia)	458
Eumenides	
Prometheus Bound	?

Sophocles   497–406

Women of Trachis	?
Ajax	before 442
Antigone	442
Oedipus Tyrannus	before 425
Electra	c. 413
Philoctetes	409
Oedipus at Colonus	405/401

Euripides   484–406

Alcestis	438
Medea	431
Children of Heracles	c. 430
Hippolytus	428
Hecabe	425
Andromache	?
Heracles	421–415
Trojan Women	415
Iphigeneia in Tauris	?
Electra	418–413
Helen	412
Ion	?
Phoenician Women	411–408
Orestes	408

Iphigeneia in Aulis	after 406
Bacchae	406
Cyclops	?
Rhoesos	?

Aristophanes 445–386

Acharnians	425
Knights	424
Clouds	423
Wasps	422
Peace	421
Birds	414
Lysistrata	411
Thesmophoriazousai	411
Frogs	405
Assembly Women	392
Wealth	388

CHAPTER FIVE

Ethics: The Philosophy of Behaviour

The Greek word *ethos* means character or disposition. It can also mean the customs or usage, the patterns of behaviour which form our characters. So ethics in the Greek sense are not to do with New Year resolutions or ideals of behaviour to which we should aspire; they deal quite simply with the ways we habitually behave. Ethics is part of philosophy and the Greeks invented both.

In any discussion of this subject, the first thing we are always told is that the word 'philosophy' is from the Greek and means 'love of wisdom (or skill)'. This is misleading, because, to most of us, 'knowledge' means simply knowing what *is*. (To know what isn't would be delusion.) So, if I know the name of the capital of Peru or the chief secretary to the Treasury, that's knowledge. And yet, philosophy doesn't deal with such matters.

In fact, philosophy doesn't seem to deal with knowing things at all, except that much of twentieth-century philosophy has spent its time arguing about what it is possible to know and whether or not it is possible to know anything. There's a story of a London taxi driver who was hailed one day by Bertrand Russell, then well known from his appearances on television. As the cab swung out into the traffic, the cabby seized his opportunity, 'Now then,' he said to the world's most famous philosopher, 'what's it all abaht, Lord Russell?' 'And, do you know?' he told his mates later, 'he couldn't tell me!'

The earliest Greek philosophers spent their time trying to find out what it's all about in the sense that they were concerned with how the world came into being, what it is ultimately made of, and why it is like it is. Because they were trying to understand an objective reality outside themselves, Thales, Anaximander and Anaximenes can be thought of as the precursors of the scientists and we have dealt with them in chapter 2. More pressing in terms of human concerns are the questions of behaviour: how should we treat each other? What is the best way for people to live together? Are right and wrong moral absolutes or do they simply reflect social customs? With these questions the greatest of Greek philosophers occupied themselves and we are still looking for the answers today.

Religion and Ethics

In the age of Homer and Hesiod, behaviour was geared to winning prestige. The hero is heroic not because he wants to be happy but because he wants to be famous. The main control on his appetite for celebrity is not a list of commandments revealed by God or the gods, but simply the fear that, if he becomes too famous, too celebrated, he might trespass on the prerogative of the gods and bring down on himself divine retribution. This is a constant theme of Greek tragedy and is simply set out by Sophocles:

For time approaching, and time hereafter,
And time forgotten, one rule stands:
That greatness never
Shall touch the life of man without destruction.   [Antigone 603 ff]

This is a formal mythical explanation of a basic human emotion we all feel: if we are too happy or successful, we had better watch out. But, apart from stepping in to pull the rug from under the man who overreaches himself, the gods did little to influence human conduct and certainly did not put themselves out to set a good example.

In fact, it was the shenanigans of the gods that caused the first open expressions of scepticism about their existence. By the sixth century, as we have seen, the thinkers of Ionia were already chipping away at the foundations of traditional beliefs. Hecataeus was the first to admit he found them 'funny' and Xenophanes attacked the morality of the myths which had Greek divinities behaving like fifth-century pop stars. He also pointed out the human tendency to create gods in their own image, which must cast doubt on their existence; but he went on to declare his own faith in a god 'who is not like men in appearance or in mind'. Xenophanes stressed that awareness of such a god is a matter of faith and not knowledge: a man might think he knows; he might even hit on the truth by accident; but he can never know that he knows [Fragment 34 quoted in Dodds 1951; p 181]. Xenophanes expressed his doubts in the Greek colonies of Southern Italy and Syracuse; back in his native Ionia his contemporaries were clearing the field for philosophical enquiry.

Heraclitus

Heraclitus was born into an aristocratic family of Ephesus around 540 and seems to have cultivated that lofty scepticism tinged with melancholy we notice cropping up in the aristocracy from Michel de Montaigne to Bertrand Russell. Heraclitus started exercising his scepticism on the common experience of dreaming, which many common people thought gave access to prophecy or to communication with the gods. He said simply that in dreams each man retreats into a world of his own. So dreams cannot be vehicles for objective truth. He went on to make fun of traditional religious rituals, saying that prayers to images were like talking to a house instead of talking to its owner and that blood purification was like trying to wash off dirt by bathing in mud. He was fond of dismissing simple beliefs of the uneducated: the whole panoply of Greek burial rites, for example, which we know from a wealth of vase painting and tragedy, he scorns with the phrase 'the dead are nastier than dung'. And as for the rich tapestry of influences − fate, luck, divine forces, birth signs − which poets, dramatists and philosophers had woven to account for what happens to a man during the course of his life, Heraclitus says simply, in three words: *ethos anthropon daimon*, 'character is destiny'. In other words, a man's fate is determined, not by outside forces but simply by the sort of man he is, the way he behaves.

This doesn't bode well for most of us because Heraclitus seems to have had a low opinion of his fellow men. As he put it, they do not know what they are doing when they are awake and forget what they are doing when they are asleep. According to the colourful but not authenticated life written by Diogenes Laertius (DK22A1) he became so misanthropic in his middle years that he took himself off to a mountain and lived on grasses and plants. His sense of superiority and mistrust of others led him to a sticky and noisome end; having contracted a dropsy he asked the doctors in a riddle if they knew how to 'make a drought out of rainy weather'. When they didn't understand what he was talking about he buried himself in a dung heap, hoping that the heat of the manure would draw off the dropsy. It didn't and he died.

Heraclitus claimed to have had no teacher and is reported to have said, when a subject needed further investigation, 'Wait a minute while I go and enquire of myself.' He seems to have cultivated a reputation for complexity which enhanced that of his intellectual superiority. Diogenes Laertius writes of his book On Nature:

He dedicated it and placed it in the temple of Artemis, as some say, having purposely written it rather obscurely so that only those of rank and influence should have access to it, and it should not be easily despised by the populace.   [IX, 5]

Even when he had a wide reputation as a sage – perhaps particularly then – Heraclitus was known as the Obscure. His sayings are certainly cryptic and have to be worked at. Here are a few of them:

The path up and down is one and the same.

An unapparent connection is stronger than an apparent one.

Thunderbolt steers all things.

It is necessary to know that war is common and right is strife and that all things happen by strife and necessity.

But, in spite of his irascible morosity, there is something compelling about Heraclitus. He realized that 'you cannot step twice into the same river'. Nothing lasts, animate or inanimate, and that reality, therefore, is a process of change: *panta rhei*, 'everything flows.' He recognized the difficulty of labelling a truth objective by pointing out that donkeys prefer rubbish to gold and men gold to rubbish; that 'the sea is the most pure and the most polluted water; for fishes it is drinkable and healthy but for men it is undrinkable and deleterious'. He made the distinction between sensation and the intelligent interpretation of sense data in the aphorism:

Evil witnesses are the eyes and ears for men, if they have souls that do not understand their language.

And finally, though he laughed at the superstitions of his day, his religious sense was acute. There is no more telling observation in the whole literature of theology on the relationship between God and man than the words of Heraclitus on the oracle at Delphi. He writes that the oracle *'oute legei, oute kruptei, alla semainei'*, that is he 'does not speak, does not hide himself, but signifies', or 'gives a sign'. So we could translate that God does not speak directly to us or hide himself from us; but he nudges our understanding.

Zeno of Elea

Zeno has always been a special favourite of mine among the Greek philosophers for reasons I'll come to in a minute, but I have to admit that he isn't generally regarded as one of the deepest. In fact his rank in the History of Greek Philosophy comes from his being the pupil and bosom friend of the great Parmenides, who stunned the nascent world of philosophical investigation with the statement 'What is, is, and what is not, is not.' Like many philosophical maxims, this one is less trite than it sounds. Parmenides was rejecting the Pythagoreans by claiming that change is an illusion; that being is, and not being is not. One cannot proceed from the other. Zeno never reached the heights of this observation but, scrabbling around as he did in the foothills, he came up with a few entertaining ideas.

These were intended to demonstrate the limitations of strictly logical reasoning and this is why Zeno has always been one of my favourites. It has been my experience that people who conduct their lives according to strictly rational principles, who submit every decision affecting their actions and relationships to the bar of reason, can still end up in the same mess as the rest of us. This often surprises strictly rational people. Zeno would have understood. A couple of his little stories illustrate:

Achilles, noted for his fleetness of foot, takes on a tortoise in a flat race. He gives the tortoise a ten-yard start. After a second he has covered five yards – half the distance between them – but the tortoise has moved on a pace and so the distance between them has changed and he hasn't quite covered half of it. Achilles will go trying to cover half the distance between them at increasing speed but, as that distance will keep changing, so will half that distance. Achilles can never catch the tortoise. He will never even get half way to catching it.

An archer shoots an arrow at a target. The arrow follows a curved line through the air. Any line is made up of a number of points. Let us consider one of them. There must be an instant of time when the arrow is neither approaching nor leaving the point. If it is neither approaching nor leaving it must be stationary. And the arrow can be similarly proved to be stationary at any, and therefore at all of the points which make up the line. So the arrow never moves.

I expect that both of these paradoxes can be explained these days by calling in the concept of space/time or some such. They must have called in question the infallibility of reason as the sole arbiter of the truth and so have an abiding value.

Sophists

As sceptics like Heraclitus, Parmenides and Zeno challenged the established values of traditional society, these values had to be replaced and, in the early fifth century, a new profession arose which claimed to be able to replace them. The early Sophists were travelling professors who, for large fees, taught a variety of subjects: ethics, politics, rhetoric, logic and grammar, all of which were originally thought to increase virtue.

Protagoras (c. 490–420), from Thrace, the earliest and most famous of the Sophists, once said to an intending pupil: 'Young man, if you come to me you will go home a better man' [quoted Grant 1989; p 71]. His belief that virtue could be taught was to be challenged by Socrates and give rise to a long and fruitful debate. But it all hangs on the use of the word 'virtue'. For Protagoras and his followers, the word 'arete', which is translated 'virtue' means 'excellence' without moral connotations. For example, the function of a knife is to cut. So, to have arete, the knife must be sharp and the most virtuous knife is the sharpest. The function of man is to be a practical success in life and so the most virtuous is the most successful. To this end, Protagoras and the Sophists taught the skills that would make a man a success, the art of getting on. Their descendants are still with us and writing best-sellers.

The best way to achieve fame in Greece at the time was through public oratory, since, as we saw in examining Athenian democracy, debates were held under the public gaze and all important decisions were taken after speeches from all sides. The Sophists taught the most effective ways to use words and, since they were selling the art of persuasion irrespective of the rights or wrongs of the case, they quickly became as rich as barristers. They were unpopular with high-minded philosophers such as Plato because they took money for their teaching and because they seemed unconcerned with right and wrong. Those who support them today point out that they were simply selling a technique and that it was not necessary that they should take a high moral tone about it. This is like saying that there's nothing wrong with guns – it's the people who shoot them. This is an attitude understandable amongst gunsmiths but questionable among moral philosophers.

But the Sophists did have a moral attitude. It didn't catch on widely in their own day but it was rediscovered and blossomed in the Renaissance and is still rampant today. Protagoras is, perhaps, most famous for his claim that 'Man is the measure of all things.' I don't think anybody really knows what this means, but it was taken up by the Renaissance humanists as meaning that humanity holds a central position in the Universe and that human aspirations are the highest at which humans should aim; Alexander Pope was to express it as:

Know then thyself, presume not God to scan.
The proper study of mankind is man.

Protagoras was certainly a humanist himself in the sense that he has doubts about the divinities. He opens his book On the Gods with the words:

With regard to the gods, I cannot feel sure either that they are or that they are not, nor what they are like in figure; for there are many things that hinder sure knowledge, the obscurity of the subject and the shortness of human life.

And he also had an optimistic view of human potentialities. He thought that, by getting rid of the old superstitions and taking on board those new insights which he and his fellow Sophists had for sale, humanity could rise to new heights of achievement. The training for virtue which a civilized society encouraged was all that was necessary. He taught that the very worst citizen of a civilized community was already a better man than the 'noble savage'. Human progress was inevitable so long as the light of education illumined the minds of men. This is a quite reasonable sales pitch for a Sophist but an unreal view of human nature.

There is another interpretation of the phrase 'Man is the measure of all things' which has always won a certain popularity and which makes ethics a waste of time. It is that all perceptions and judgements are relative; that what I perceive to be right is right for me; that right and wrong have no more ultimate validity than sweet and sour. This was not taught by Protagoras, who saw the value of established laws and customs, but it was quickly picked up by his followers and has served to make his name popular in those easy riding schools of philosophy which teach that the right thing to do in all situations is your own thing and that the finest epitaph to which we can aspire is 'I did it My Way.'

The Sophists tended to avoid ultimate ethical principles and teach simply that competency in argument was independent of the merits of the case being argued. They developed eye-catching ways of showing off their skills, one of which was to argue strongly in favour of a proposition and then just as persuasively against it. What they sought to demonstrate was that it is not the truth of a proposition which recommends it to an audience but the skill with which it is presented. This was the skill they had for sale.

The most successful of the Sophists in their own terms was Gorgias who did not arrive in Athens until he was fifty-five years old but then dazzled the Athenians by the richness of his robe and the expense of his lifestyle. This means that he must have already made his packet back in his native Leontini, in Sicily. He was so rich that he presented the oracle at Delphi with a life-size gold statue of himself to thank the god Apollo for the natural gifts which had produced all this money. He must have had what today goes by the name of a charismatic personality and great stage presence as he strode into the theatre and shouted to the audience to 'Give me a theme!' Rather strangely, his basic philosophy, outlined in his book On Nature or the Non-Existent consisted of three propositions: 1. Nothing exists. 2. If anything does exist it can't be known and 3. If anybody does know what exists he can't communicate it to anybody else. Nobody is quite sure whether this was a serious doctrine of philosophical Nihilism or a joke to demonstrate that a skilful rhetorician could argue in favour of the daftest ideas. What we do know is that Gorgias claimed the only important thing in life was the power of persuasion and that this should be cultivated and used for its own sake, unmuddied by considerations as to the truth or falsity of the argument.

Other Sophists who made a comfortable living were Thrasymachus of Chalcedon who is represented by Plato in the Republic as the champion of the superior rights of the stronger, and Antiphon of Athens who had the gall to denounce the difference between noble and common, Greek and barbarian, and say that education made the distinctions. He was also famous for teaching that he could cure the depressed by his skill with words.

The Classical Philosophers

The Professor of Moral Philosophy at the University of Oxford, Bernard Williams, might reasonably be supposed to know what he's talking about when it comes to estimating the importance of the Greeks to his subject. And he doesn't mess about: 'The legacy of the Greeks to Western Philosophy', he once wrote, 'is – Western Philosophy'. When I asked him to explain this, he pointed out that in the case of the sciences and certain forms of literature, the Greeks started things off but a great deal of what has happened since has left the Greeks behind. If you have to explain the origins of a modern scientific theory or a play of Shakespeare, you have to mention a lot of influences apart from the Greeks. In fact you needn't mention the Greeks at all. But the peculiarity of philosophy is that not only were its main areas of interest laid down by the Greeks, but their contribution was and is so important that anybody who studies the subject today will be studying the texts of, for example, Plato and Aristotle as an essential part of their course.

This is not because the Greeks played an important part in the History of Philosophy, but because what they had to say is still relevant to the subject today. It may seem odd to suggest that, in an advanced industrial society with all the new and sophisticated pressures generated by twentieth-century life, there can be any application today of the moral principles worked out in an eastern Mediterranean town over two and a half thousand years ago; but there are certain fundamental distinctions which have to be used in thinking about morality: virtue, character, law, the good, which were carved out by the Greeks and are presented by them in ways which are interesting, challenging, and so fundamental that they apply across time and cultures.

Socrates

I still have a T-shirt which was a gift from the producer and staff of the BBC programmes *Everyman* and *Heart of the Matter* when I stopped work as presenter. On the chest are the words I'M JUST TRYING

TO UNDERSTAND. It seems I used this phrase a lot. Both programmes involved interviews 'in depth', as they say in the media, with rather impressive people. Now, one way of tackling an impressive person on television is to make it clear that you're not impressed; you bark out a few aggressive questions you've worked out with your research team, interrupt the answers, and if serious points are being made in reply, react by shaking the head silently with a smile of disbelief. The main object is to make it clear to the viewers that you're giving the impressive person a hard time. In this way brilliant careers have been made and choleric television presenters have become household names.

Sadly, I was always too short on aplomb to carry off this technique. So I fell back on doing what came naturally when faced by people who knew far more than I did, which was to try to understand them, to ask them to explain their point of view. It only emerged later that this approach, the last refuge of timidity, was just as effective as the pugnacity of my more eminent colleagues in collapsing stout parties because, if there is no acceptable explanation for a point of view, the best way to reveal this is to ask for one. I had, of course, stumbled on the oldest interviewing technique of all time. Its inventor would certainly have won a chat show on television today; in his own age they ordered things differently and he was sentenced to death.

Socrates is most famous for revealing to impressive people that they knew rather less than they thought they did. He approached his task by a series of questions which seemed to be simply part of a search for greater enlightenment. When a famous general spoke of bravery, a subject in which he might be expected to have taken a certain professional interest, Socrates asks for more information:

Socrates: *Very well, let us take as an example the brave man you have mentioned, the man who keeps his position in the line and fights the enemy.*

Lakhes: *Yes, he is a brave man.*

Socrates: *I agree. But what about the man who fights the enemy not by keeping the position but by retreating?*

Lakhes: *What do you mean, retreating?*

Socrates: *I'm thinking of the Scythians who are said to fight as much by withdrawing*

> as by pursuing ... For I wanted to get your opinion not only of bravery in the hoplite line, but also in cavalry engagements and in all forms of fighting; and indeed of bravery not only in fighting but also at sea, and in the face of illness and poverty and public affairs. And there is bravery not only in face of pain and fear but also of desire and pleasure, both fearsome to fight against whether by attack or retreat — for some men are brave in these encounters, aren't they, Lakhes?

Lakhes: [who must be feeling the subject is slipping away from him] Yes, certainly.

Socrates: Then all these are examples of bravery, only some men show it in pleasure, some in pain, some in desire, some in danger. And there are others who show cowardice in the same circumstances.

Lakhes: Yes.

Socrates: Now what I want to know is just what each of these two qualities is. So try again and tell me first, what is this common characteristic of courage which they all share? Do you understand now what I mean?

Lakhes: I'm afraid I don't.

[PLATO, Lakhes 191a, QUOTED JACT 1984; PP 294-5]

Everybody who writes about Socrates has to make the point that he wrote nothing himself and that all we know about him comes from his admirers Xenophon and Plato (apart from his brief appearance as a comic character in Aristophanes). Now, as Xenophon was a country gentleman rather keen on hunting, horsemanship and estate management, he may well have had the same rather limited intellectual curiosity as our own country squires. In other words, he may not have been entirely sure what Socrates was on about and indeed his misunderstanding of Socrates seems to be as profound as his admiration. Plato presents a problem in the other direction: being a creative writer and thinker he may well have credited Socrates with his own ideas. These problems have led scholars to doubt that we can ever really come to know Socrates. All I can say here is that, to me, he is one of the most powerfully alive characters in the whole of human history and that, although most of this power comes from the writings of Plato, those writings were in circulation whilst hundreds of admirers of Socrates were still alive which may be some reassurance as to their substantial truth.

Socrates was a lover of life and we hear of him eating and drinking with the best, though he was never drunk. People compared him to Silenus, who almost always was, so the comparison must have had to do with his appearance rather than his sobriety. Silenus, the tutor and companion of Dionysus, was short, fat, bald and ugly.

Socrates loved a party but would also stand alone and motionless from one dawn to the next if a thought struck him and he needed to work it out. As a soldier, he had shown great courage and hardiness:

On one occasion in particular, when there was a tremendous frost and everybody either remained indoors or, if they did go out muffled themselves up as never before and tied up their feet in sheepskins, Socrates went out wearing only his ordinary clothes and with nothing at all on his feet and walked over the ice barefoot . . .   [PLATO, Symposium 219-20]

Socrates was a practical man and yet a mystic, a sociable man and yet a recluse, a sensualist and yet an ascetic, a sceptic and yet driven by a mystical vision of human capabilities. It is hard for really superior men to be lovable, but Socrates somehow managed it.

Socrates described himself as not an original thinker but a sort of intellectual midwife:

My art of midwifery is concerned with men and not women and I am concerned with minds in travail and not with bodies. And the most important thing about my art is its ability to test fully whether the mind of the young man is giving birth to a mere image and a falsehood or to a legitimate truth. For there is another point I have in common with the midwives — I cannot myself give birth to wisdom, and the criticism which is often made of me that though I ask questions of others I have no wisdom in me, is quite true. The reason is that god compels me to be midwife but forbids me to give birth. So I am myself quite without wisdom nor has my mind produced any original thought; but those who keep my company, though at first some of them may appear quite ignorant, if god wills, in due course make what both they and others think is marvellous progress. This is clearly not because of anything they have learned from me but because they have made many marvellous discoveries of themselves and given birth to them. But the delivery of them is my work and god's . . .   [PLATO, Theaitetos 150b, QUOTED JACT 1984; PP295-6]

Socrates was more than the inventor of an effective interview technique; there was more to him than the sceptic. He saw himself as a man with a mission and once described how that mission began. One of his disciples asked the Delphic oracle whether there was anyone wiser than Socrates – which implies, of course, that he had already acquired a reputation for wisdom – and the oracle said there was not. Socrates tells us, in the *Apology*, that he then set out on a search to prove the oracle wrong by finding somebody wiser than himself. He could only find people who thought they were wise and came to the conclusion that the oracle must mean that his superiority lay simply in the fact that he, at least, knew he was not.

Of course there's a touch of irony here; but the mission he speaks of was so important to him that he was to choose death rather than abandon it. There must have been a more positive cause than the mere shattering of complacency, vital though that process is in the search for truth.

Socrates had a conviction that there is such a thing as an absolute and unchanging standard – of truth, justice, right as opposed to wrong – and that it is our duty to try to discover it and to lead our lives as closely as possible in conformity with it. This made him question particularly those who were guilty of what Sartre called 'bad faith' – people who act without admitting, or perhaps recognizing, the real motives behind their actions. He believed that we can be as precise about our moral behaviour as about practical skills such as carpentry and that the job of the philosopher is to seek after that precision by analysing moral language and spotting its defects and confusions. His main attacks were launched against sloppy thinking and moral relativism.

The most consistent positive thrust of Socrates' teaching was that men should care for their souls. Now, today, that phrase has become emptied of meaning through overuse and if it still carries any overtones for us at all they have to do with securing a better place in the afterlife through avoiding certain activities in this one – such as sex before marriage or mowing the lawn on Sundays. But Socrates was using the word 'soul' with a special significance. For him, the soul was the central essence of a person, that which made him what he was. This was a new doctrine. The soul had previously been thought to be either the breath of life which a man gives up when he dies, or an imprisoned piece of divinity which is released from the body at death. If, as Socrates taught, the soul is the essential self, then it follows that, the soul being virtuous, a person will behave well so long as he has knowledge and freedom of choice. This explains one of the more puzzling and apparently wrong tenets of Socrates: that a man will behave well if he has knowledge. Our everyday experience teaches us that we can be aware of the right action and choose the wrong. In fact we would say that a person is fully to blame for a wrong action only if he performs it with full knowledge of its wrongness. But Socrates says that wisdom and virtue are one, so that a wise man, that is one who knows what is right, will also do what is right. Nobody chooses to do evil as such, with full knowledge of the nature of the act. This seems to overlook the irrational as a force in determining human conduct. But Socrates could well have held that the irrational clouds the understanding and so prevents that knowledge of the right which leads to right action.

The trial and death of Socrates have been much debated. He was charged with not believing in the gods of the state, with introducing new gods, and with corrupting the young. It seems so obviously a situation of flagrant injustice that it is not easy to understand how he could have been convicted in a city so obsessed by democratic ideals which did not insist on religious conformity. But it may help to remember that Athens had been humiliated by defeat in the Peloponnesian war, that the people who convicted Socrates had seen their city starved and crushed by the Spartans; that the man who had most helped the enemy was Alcibiades, a close friend of Socrates, and that the bloodthirsty group set up in Athens by the Spartans had been led by Critias, another. There must have been many who felt that a time of war is not the time to challenge the social and political institutions of a society under threat. Socrates, although a loyal citizen, did exactly that, publicly and consistently. It is true that he had made many enemies amongst men with a reputation for wisdom who had argued with him and come off second best, but it is not true, as is sometimes suggested, that they led an ignorant mob to condemn him. The situation was closer to Greek tragedy than to the Western: there was right on both sides.

He was found guilty by a majority of 281 votes to 220. The penalty of death was demanded by the prosecution and it was left to Socrates to propose an alternative. If he had chosen to be banished, the jury would certainly have agreed with the consent of the prosecution who sought to silence as much as to punish him. But Socrates had another idea:

What do I deserve to suffer, or pay? My life has not been a quiet one, despite my disregard for the things that most men care about: making money, running a household, holding high military or domestic posts, and all the other things – offices clubs, intrigues – that go on in our polis; I thought that I was really too upright to survive if I went in for all that. So instead of embarking on a course which would have benefited neither you nor myself, I set myself instead the task of benefiting each one of you in the very best way that I know how: I tried to persuade each one of you not to put personal advantage before personal well being – that is, becoming as good and wise a man as possible – and not to put advantage before well being in the case of the polis either, or in anything else. What, then, do I deserve to suffer for behaving in this way? If I would be truthful about my deserts, Athenians, nothing could be more suitable for such a man than [free] maintenance at public expense; at least he deserves it more than your Olympic victors do ... Such men give you the appearance of good fortune, I the reality; and I need the support, not they. So if I am obliged to propose a penalty, which is both appropriate and just, this is it – [free] maintenance at public expense.

[PLATO, *Apology* 35e–37e QUOTED CRAWFORD & WHITEHEAD 1983; PP 470-1]

The jury were so insulted at the suggestion that a convicted criminal should be maintained at the State's expense that, even when Socrates had been persuaded by his friends to suggest a fine, they voted for the death penalty by 360 to 140: a larger majority than had originally convicted him. The story of the trial, which is told in Plato's *Apology*, has Socrates as its hero: cool, rational, superior to his accusers. The reader feels squarely on his side and, perhaps just a touch of hesitation when Socrates insists that he must continue his mission because it is god-given and god-directed. Only in this aspect of his personality does he seem to depart from the humble, rational, self-effacing seeker after the truth.

But, in the Crito and the Phaedo, which describe his last days in prison and his death, Socrates is compelling and it is difficult to read the final pages without tears.

He could not be executed immediately after the trial because the annual mission to the sacred island of Delos in honour of the god Apollo had not returned and the custom was that, during its absence, no executions would take place. At the beginning of Crito, Socrates is visited, before dawn, by his friend Crito, who sits by his sleeping form until he wakes. He has bribed the jailer to let him in, he says, but he brings bad news; the ship from Delos has been seen rounding the point of Sunium and will soon be in Athens. There are only a few hours left. Crito had done a deal with the warders to let Socrates escape and his friends have all agreed to chip in with the money. Socrates is interested but points out that, since he has spent his life trying to avoid doing wrong, it is important not to be deflected from this by the accident of his being imprisoned and condemned to death. So he proposes that they discuss the rightness of an attempt to break out of prison before they make it. They begin by agreeing that to do wrong is, in every sense, bad:

Socrates: *Then in no circumstances must one do wrong.*

Crito: *No.*

Socrates: *In that case one must not even do wrong when one is wronged, which most people regard as the natural course.*

Crito: *Apparently not.*

Socrates: *Tell me another thing,*

Crito: *Ought one to do injuries or not?*

Crito: *Surely not, Socrates.*

Socrates: *And tell me: is it right to do an injury in retaliation, as most people believe, or not?*

Crito: *No, never.*   [PLATO 1969; P 88]

Crito has already lost the argument and Socrates goes on to point out that an honourable man must obey the law even when its judgement goes against him because otherwise the law would be destroyed by the whims of private persons. He is ready to listen to any counter-arguments which Crito proposes, but Crito gives up.

The execution has to take place the following day and Socrates is surrounded by his friends for his last hours. They begin a discussion on the nature of death:

I suppose that for one who is soon to leave this world there is no more suitable occupation than inquiring into our views about the future life, and trying to imagine what it is like. What else can one do in the time before sunset? [IBID; P 104]

They discuss the possibility of a continued existence after death and ask whether a wise man, on the knowledge we have, should welcome the prospect. Socrates thinks that the quality of life after death has something to do with a man's character. What he says is: 'I have a firm hope that there is something in store for those who have died, and (as we have been told for many years) something much better for the good than for the wicked.'

The discussion turns into an argument and Socrates, who notices that Crito has been trying for some time to get a word in, asks him to speak:

'Only this, Socrates,' said Crito, 'that the man who is to give you the poison has been asking me for a long time to tell you to talk as little as possible; he says that talking makes you heated, and that you ought not to do anything to affect the action of the poison. Otherwise it is sometimes necessary to take a second dose or even a third.'

'That is his affair,' said Socrates. 'Let him make his own preparations for administering it twice or three times if necessary.' [IBID; P 107]

The most interesting philosophical problem as Socrates and his friends wait for the time to drink the poison is whether or not the soul is immortal. Socrates says it is and tries to prove it by a series of arguments. The first is that everything is generated from its opposite: so the weaker comes from the stronger and the faster from the slower. And since everything which is dead has once been alive, it follows that the living come into being from the dead. Therefore the souls must continue to exist in another world. He backs this argument up with his theory that what we think we learn in this world is in fact recollection of what we already know. He has demonstrated this in the past in conversation with a slave who knew no geometry but, answering questions put to him by Socrates who drew a number of diagrams to explain the questions, managed to solve a geometrical problem. Since people are able to answer questions correctly on subjects they have not learned, it follows that they must possess knowledge of these subjects at birth. This knowledge, therefore, must have been acquired by the soul in a previous existence. Therefore the soul is immortal.

The arguments of Socrates are convincing to those who already accept their conclusions and are mainly compelling as an illustration of the kind of man he was and the way in which he faced death still encouraging his friends and searching after truth. He insists repeatedly on the importance of the philosopher's approach to life – the rejection of the pleasures of the body in favour of care of the soul. And he justifies it with a view of what happens after death to the person who is attached to worldly things:

> ... if at the time of its release the soul is tainted and impure, because it has always associated with the body and cared for it and loved it, and has always been so beguiled by the body and its passions and pleasures that nothing seems real to it but those physical things which can be touched and seen and eaten and drunk and used for sexual enjoyment; and if it is accustomed to hate and fear and avoid what is invisible and hidden from our eyes, but intelligible and comprehensible by philosophy – if the soul is in this state, do you think it will escape independent and uncontaminated? [IBID; P133]

He goes on to speak of the underworld, and of the boiling lake of muddy water into which the river Acheron discharges itself with great sheets of fire and jets of lava. Here the evil are punished and the good pass upward to a pure abode to live a beautiful existence without bodies. Socrates then seems to catch himself out in a bout of unphilosophical romanticizing and says: 'Of course, no reasonable man ought to insist that the facts are exactly as I have described them.' But he goes on to say that a belief in some such post-mortem scenario is good for the self-confidence of the philosopher. It's a foretaste of Pascal's famous wager.

Suddenly, at this point, Socrates decides to bathe: 'I prefer to have a bath before drinking the poison, rather than giving the women the trouble of washing me when I am dead.' This switch to direct practical matters prompts Crito to ask Socrates how he would like to be buried. Socrates answers with a touch of impatience that he has clearly been wasting his time with the long explanation of how his soul is about to be separated from his body. Crito can, of course, do what he likes with the body, since Socrates will no longer be in it.

The prison officer enters and says:

Socrates, at any rate I shall not have to find fault with you, as I do with others, for getting angry with me and cursing when I tell them to drink the poison — carrying out Government orders. I have come to know during this time that you are the noblest and the gentlest and the bravest of all the men that have ever come here... [IBID; P 180]

And he stammers out a 'Goodbye', bursts into tears and runs away.

Then Socrates asks Crito to send for the slave with the poison, if it is prepared; 'if not, tell the man to prepare it.'

'But surely, Socrates,' said Crito, 'the sun is still upon the mountains; it has not gone down yet. Besides, I know that in other cases people have dinner and enjoy their wine and sometimes the company of those whom they love, long after they receive the warning; and only drink the poison quite late at night. No need to hurry; there is still plenty of time.' [IBID; P 181]

But Socrates replies that such behaviour is natural for people with a great attachment to life, whereas he, by putting off the poison until the last minute would gain nothing and only make himself look ridiculous in his own eyes 'if I clung to life and hugged it when it has no more to offer.'

The slave enters with the poison and Socrates asks him, calmly:

'Well, my good fellow, you understand these things; what ought I to do?'

'Just drink it', he said, 'and then walk about until you feel a weight in your legs, and then lie down. Then it will act of its own accord.' [IBID; PP 181-2]

Socrates asks if he may pour a libation from the cup, but the man says that they prepare only a normal dose. So, with a brief prayer to the gods, Socrates quite calmly and with no sign of distaste, drains the poison in one draught. His friends burst into tears, Apollodorus so passionately that everyone breaks down. Socrates protests:

Really, my friends, what a way to behave! Why, that was my main reason for sending away the women, to prevent this sort of disturbance. [IBID; P 182]

And he urges them to be calm and brave. He walks around the cell a little and then, his legs feeling heavy, lies down. The slave examines his feet and legs and then pinches his foot hard and asks if he feels anything. Socrates says 'No'. Then he does the same to the legs and slowly moving upwards, demonstrates that the body is getting cold and numb. When the numbness reaches the heart, he explains, Socrates will be dead. As the numbness reaches the waist, Socrates, who had covered his own face, uncovers it and says, with, possibly, a final touch of irony:

Crito, we ought to offer up a cock to Asclepius. See to it, and don't forget.

[IBID; P 183]

Asclepius was the god of healing. The cock was an offering in gratitude for a cure effected; death is the cure for life. Crito assures him the offering will be made and asks if there is anything else which must be done.

There is no reply.

Plato

One of the problems we keep coming across with the early philosophers is that, as they wrote nothing, like Socrates, or almost nothing has survived, like most of the others, we have to guess at what they taught from what others wrote about them. Plato is different. He wrote a lot. And a lot has survived: about twice as much as Homer. We know so much about what he had to say that Alfred Whitehead characterized the whole European philosophical tradition as merely 'a series of footnotes to Plato'.

We know rather less about his life than we might think we do, because biographies have been constructed on insufficient evidence by highly imaginative writers. We are not even sure of the date of his birth. Greeks were understandably incurious about this when you come to think that few people achieve much in the first few years of their lives. It's more interesting to know when they were at their peak and this is what Greeks normally remembered. With Plato there's another problem since his peak turned out to be a high plateau and he was up there for about forty years.

He was born, probably in 429, into an aristocratic Athenian family, which traced its origins on both sides to royalty. (It will help to remember this when we come to hear about his social attitudes.) He was, in his youth, besotted by Socrates and was probably about thirty-one years old when his master was forced to drink the hemlock. Plato then left Athens in disgust, staying for a time in Megara, where there were other devotees of Socrates, and then setting off for a long period of travel to Egypt, Italy and Sicily. He may have served for a period in the Athenian army but it was not until he was in his early forties that he settled again in Athens and began teaching. In 387 he founded the Academy outside Athens which we heard about earlier and began a system of instruction which has been called the first university. It seems to have been more relaxed and pastoral than most of our universities – even including those informal foundations along the west coast of the United States – because the method of instruction was mainly through conversations in which students and teacher sought the truth together. The main areas of study were Astronomy and Mathematics. Over the door of the Academy were inscribed the words *Medeis Ageometretos Eisito*, which have been translated 'A Credit in Mathematics is required'. The study of mathematics was for Plato rather like the study of Plato is for our classical teachers: it trained the mind in the processes of logical thought. Plato taught at the Academy for the rest of his life, close to a shrine of the Muses, and was buried there when he died in his eighty-second year.

One incident in an otherwise peaceful academic life is of interest: whilst on his travels, Plato had met, befriended and impressed Dion, the son-in-law of Dionysius, tyrant of Syracuse in Sicily. When the tyrant died, Dion invited Plato to Syracuse to educate the heir Dionysius II so that the country might have the benefit of a philosopher-king to rule with that benevolent despotism all right-thinking Platonists preached. Sadly, Plato and his pupil did not get on, possibly because Plato insisted that the first essential of statecraft was a mastery of geometry and his pupil failed to grasp its relevance or to work up the necessary enthusiasm and staying power in that subject. Dionysius decided that he could rule perfectly well without either knowing or being able to prove the relationship between the square on the hypotenuse of a right-angled triangle and that on the other two sides and Plato went back home.

The incident shows that Plato was a practical philosopher; he really believed that the study of philosophy could lead men to behave better towards each other and to organize themselves better in society. We hear much about the idealism of Plato and of his metaphysics, which we'll come to in a moment, but he was as concerned with present as with ultimate realities, and a lot of hard work and thought went into designing ways in which people could live together.

When we come to look at these it's helpful to remember two things; firstly that, as new colonies were still being founded in Plato's time, it was perfectly practical to work out new social systems with a real possibility that they could be tried out but, secondly, Plato had a subtle sense of irony and we can't always be sure, when he puts forward an outrageous solution, that he isn't, anticipating Jonathan Swift, just drawing attention to a problem.

His best known proposals for a new social order are in the Republic but he revised them later in life and produced, in his Laws, a final and less idealized version of his perfect city. Because the Laws were the outcome of mature reflection it is to them, rather than the better-known Republic that we should refer if we want to be fair to Plato. But the Laws is, admittedly, less entertaining – there's no story-line to speak of – and it is the longest work Plato ever wrote.

It was written from the Academy, where Plato had founded a school of Jurisprudence to which Greek states would commonly apply for the drafting of their legislation or for new codes of law when new colonies were being founded. 'There is no more useful corrective of the popular notion of Plato as an unpractical visionary', wrote a historian of Greek philosophy, 'than the careful study of the dullest and most technical parts of the *Laws*...' [John Burnet, quoted in Livingstone 1921; p 84].

Now it is fair, at this point, to ask why we should tackle it at all; those of us, that is, who are neither about to set off and found new colonies nor are set alight by Political Science as a lively way to occupy the mind. The answer is that, in writing about how people should organize themselves in societies, Plato reveals his deepest thoughts about what people are like: what is, or should be, important to us; what are our strengths and weaknesses, our most basic hopes and fears. And, when Plato thinks deeply about anything, it's well worth lending an ear.

In the *Republic*, Plato had put forward the idea that the best people to rule the state would be the philosophers, since ruling with justice demands thought and philosophers are the people best equipped to think. They should be selected and specially trained to be the disinterested guardians of the people. But in the *Laws*, he has come to realize the problems of handing over the government to an enclosed élite and he abandons the rule by philosophers to replace it by that of the middle class. Realizing that the well-to-do resent being put on an equal basis with the poor, he weights their political influence – much as it was weighted in the slow struggle towards democracy in Britain when there was for many years a property-owning qualification for the right to vote.

Plato acknowledged that the most basic problem in attempting to organize a community of people to live and work together is how to make them good. We have the same problem today and tend to approach it by increasing the numbers and the pay of our police force. Plato held that the philosophically inclined could find the good through dialogue with each other, seeking the truth dispassionately through rational discourse; but this had the disadvantage of taking a long time, there was no guarantee they would find it at the end, and not everybody was philosophically inclined or could find the time to wander about chatting. The common man wants to be happy; Plato wanted him to be good. So the shortest way to persuade him to be good is to convince him that happiness and goodness go together. Plato himself believed this to be true but knew that it might be difficult to sell the idea widely.

By the time he wrote the Laws, Plato had come to a settled unvarnished view of human nature in the light of experience. He saw man as a puppet, a creature on a string whose hopes and fears, pleasures and pains, appetites and passions make it jerk mindlessly about. This view has been put down by some scholars to an embittered senility but is surely not far removed from that currently held by those healthy young people who make our television advertisements.

Plato had no television but he did have available that other force which used to shape people's lives and characters in the pre-television age: religion. And he saw that religion could become a social institution which could be used to improve behaviour. So he goes to some length in the Laws to prove the existence of the gods, their inescapable justice and their constant interest in human affairs. He includes these propositions in the legal code with penalties for those who propagate disbelief in them, including the death penalty for the persistent offenders. Religious instruction was to be a compulsory subject for all children.

Before getting carried away on a wave of indignation at these outrageous interferences in basic human freedoms, it's worth looking at the religion on which Plato sought to base his ideal city.

The first thing we have to admit is that it was a great improvement on the popular religion of his day and he introduced some basic and important reforms. The gods were to be a joint cult between Apollo, the traditional focus of worship for the masses, and Helios, the sun god, representing the natural religion of the philosophers. The important new emphasis in the Laws is that these gods would not take bribes.

Plato realized that there were practitioners of the religion of his time who were a threat to public morality: the travelling priests and diviners who specialized in rituals for purifying sinners or organizing sacrifices which would produce specific benefits. He attacked such people, who have in all ages preyed on superstition, by pointing out that the gods were incorruptible. This meant that their justice would not be swayed by gifts and that private sacrifice in gratitude for future favours, a traditional practice of great antiquity, was a waste of time.

Another great reform was in his insistence on personal accountability for doing wrong. The idea that divine justice was visited on the descendants of the wrongdoer was offensive to Plato and he insists, in a remarkable passage which has echoes down the centuries from Christopher Marlowe to Jean-Paul Sartre, that retribution takes the form of a sort of spiritual gravitation. Every soul naturally gravitates, in this life, to the company of its own kind. So that, in the life or lives to come, it will have determined the company it keeps. And therein lies the punishment or the reward. Hell, Plato seems to hint, is a state of mind:

And in spite of your belief that the gods neglect you, my lad ... 'This is the sentence of the gods that dwell upon Olympus' — to go to join worse souls as you grow worse and better souls as you grow better, and alike in life and all the deaths you suffer to do and be done by according to the standards that birds of a feather naturally apply among themselves. Neither you nor anyone else who has got into trouble will ever be able to run fast enough to boast that he has escaped this sentence.   [PLATO 1975; P439]

There would, of course, be crime even in the perfect city and Plato goes into the matter of culpability and of punishment at some length. His views have a contemporary ring at odds with his reactionary and right-wing image. Plato would have sympathized, for example, with those amongst our social workers who hold that crime is committed by the socially deprived out of the desperation brought about by their circumstances. He thought, as did Socrates, that nobody ever does wrong of their own free will:

The origin of crimes is passion, desire, or ignorance, so that, only when the soul is clouded or the mind uninstructed, will people do wrong.

His laws all have a persuasive preamble in which their intention is made clear. Plato realized that it is far better to persuade the citizens that crime is wrong, so that they will avoid it, than to punish them after they have committed one. But he recognizes that injuries will be done and so there must be punishment as compensation and to encourage reformation. He insists that 'admonition should precede punishment'.

Education is to be the instrument of social stability and it begins before birth: pregnant women are to be 'carefully tended and kept from violent or excessive pleasures or pains: and at that time should cultivate gentleness and benevolence'. Infancy, which lasts for three years, is the time to lay the foundations of character by getting rid of the self-will in the child. This should be done by 'punishing him, not so as to disgrace him.' Again, Plato seems to anticipate modern psychology by stressing the importance of play:

... no-one, in any state, has really grasped that children's games affect legislation so crucially as to determine whether the laws that are passed will survive or not.

This turns out to have less to do with training in the formal release of aggression or the sublimation of the sex drive than respect for established institutions:

If you control the way children play, and the same children play the same games under the same rules and in the same conditions, and get pleasure from the same toys, you'll find that the conventions of adult life too are left in peace without alteration ... [the man who introduces new games] is the biggest menace that can ever afflict a state, because he quietly changes the character of the young by making them despise old things and value novelty.   [IBID; P 283]

Up to the age of six, children are to be educated in games and educated together. After that time the sexes are to be separated, but Plato stresses that this does not mean inequality of education. Women are capable of following the same careers as men and should be trained to do so. Failure to realize this is not only socially but economically ridiculous:

Almost every state, under present conditions, is only half a state, and develops only half its potentialities, whereas with the same cost and effort, it could double its achievement. Yet what a staggering blunder for a legislator to make!   [IBID; P 294]

In fact he stresses that girls are to be taught the same things as boys, to undergo military training with them and even to perform a military dance in a full suit of armour. Dancing is important in education, as training both the body and the mind. The music forms the mind, and the body, by being made to execute movements gracefully, is brought under full control. As for the other arts, Plato is cautious about them and his insistence on censorship has made his views unacceptable in our own time. But what he has to say may have some relevance to the effects we experience of competition in the media to increase ratings:

Pleasure is indeed a proper criterion in the arts, but not the pleasure experienced by anybody and everybody ... For instance, the law now in force in Sicily and Italy, by truckling to the majority of the audience and deciding the winner by a show of hands, has had a disastrous effect on the authors themselves, who compose to gratify the depraved tastes of their judges; the result is that in effect they are taught by the audience. It has been equally disastrous for the quality of the pleasure felt by the spectators ...   [IBID; P 95]

As for property, Plato abandons the communism of the Republic and allows personal property, although no family should accumulate more than four times as much as any other. He has a deep mistrust of wealth and has lived long enough to realize that its pursuit is at the heart of most of the ills of society. He accepts that a good man can possess a moderate amount of wealth, but states in the most unambiguous language that the very wealthy cannot be morally superior:

I mean, it's pretty well inevitable that happiness and virtue should come hand in hand (and this is the situation the legislator will want to see), but virtue and great wealth are quite incompatible, at any rate great wealth as generally understood (most people will think of the extreme case of a millionaire, who will of course be a rogue into the bargain). In view of all this, I'll never concede ... that the rich man can become really happy without being virtuous as well: to be extremely virtuous and exceptionally rich at the same time is absolutely out of the question.   [IBID; P 212]

He goes on to explain that the most wealthy cannot be virtuous because riches which come from sources that are both just and unjust will always exceed those which are confined to sources which are only just. This, though unprovable in practice, seems quite likely.

It is, of course, in his lofty and dismissive view of 'the many' that Plato jars on us today. Left to their own devices, he believes, the majority of people would behave selfishly and would be destructive of the common good. They have to be educated, coerced if necessary into decent behaviour. The methods of coercion have been described as 'an appalling control system' which 'chills one's blood' [Levi 1985; p 355] and our experience of the ways in which totalitarian regimes have operated in our own lifetime must make us feel revulsion at their being seriously proposed. But the human weaknesses they seek to correct are still with us. That Plato was so sensitive to them is part of his greatness. And we are no closer than he was to a solution.

At the basis of his attitude to mankind in general was an instinct which has found expression in similar words down the centuries from Marcus Aurelius to T. S. Eliot:

Human kind
Cannot bear very much reality.
[Four Quartets: Burnt Norton 1]

Plato's most famous image of this situation is that of the cave where men are lying, their necks and legs in chains, from their early childhood. The chains on their necks prevent them from turning their heads, so they can only see the back wall of the cave. There is a fire burning outside the cave and a wall that runs between the fire and the opening of the cave 'like the screens which showmen have in front of the audience, over which they show the puppets'. From time to time, men walk along the side of the wall carrying objects – statues, shapes of men and other creatures – which project over the top of the wall and so cast shadows, thrown by the firelight, onto the back of the cave. These carriers occasionally speak to each other and their words echo from the back wall of the cave and seem to be coming from the shadows. Because the prisoners can see only these shadows and hear only these echoes for the whole of their lives, they know no other reality.

It's always helpful to think of Plato's cave after watching news and current affairs on television. Because we're shown pictures, like the shadows on the cave wall, which we accept as reality when, in fact, they are edited representations of incidents which reporters, news editors, press agencies and channel controllers happen to think are significant. Our notions of the way the world is are shaped by shadows manipulated by the mass media who are operating not out of a dispassionate love of communicating the truth but because they need viewers, listeners, or readers. This isn't the place for a diatribe on the presentation of news and current affairs in the mass media; but the image of Plato's cave in the mind helps us to realize, when we hear the words 'and that's the World this Weekend', that, of course, it isn't.

The allegory of the cave continues with the fate of the prophet: the man who escapes and stumbles out of the entrance to the cave into the real world. After being dazzled by the light of the fire, he slowly comes to see and understand the true reality of which his companions see only the shadows. And if he should return, out of compassion for them, to the darkness of the cave and try to persuade them that they were looking at shadows:

... would not men laugh at him and say that, having gone up above he had come back with his sight ruined, so that it was not worth while even to try to go up? And do you not think that they would kill him who tried to release them and bear them up, if they could lay hands on him and slay him?   [QUOTED LOWES DICKINSON 1947; P 152]

There is so much in Plato to delight the mind and stretch the imagination, both in his insights into human psychology and his speculations about ultimate reality. Plato was a great and imaginative writer so that to read him, even in translation, is an exciting experience. There is always the underlying feeling that the realities he is dealing with are only shadows of those that exist in the transcendent world. For many people, down the centuries, his speculations about the possible nature of that transcendent world and our present and ultimate relationship with it are his finest contribution to human thought. But not to his most distinguished pupil.

Aristotle

Aristotle was born at Stagirus, a colony of Ionians settled in Chalcidice, and his father was physician to the king. At the age of seventeen, he was sent to Plato's Academy at Athens to study and he stayed there for the next twenty years, as student and teacher. He developed under the teaching of Plato to be a close associate and, since he broke away from his master and has often been contrasted with him, it's startling to think that Aristotle was closer to Plato than Plato had been to Socrates. When Plato died, he moved away and settled for a time in Asia Minor, where he married the ward of a tyrant, and then on the island of Lesbos, from where he was recalled to Macedonia by Philip II to take charge of the education of his son Alexander who later became the Great.

We have no evidence of whether they got on better than Plato and Dionysius – in fact the evidence for the appointment isn't all that good – but it came to an end long before Alexander became king and Aristotle probably went back home to Stagirus. Five years later he returned to Athens at the age of about forty-nine and founded the Lyceum which was a more formal educational institution than Plato's Academy. Here he gave lectures and supervised research on a vast range of subjects until the death of Alexander, when the Athenians had the courage to show their anti-Macedonian feelings. Like Socrates, Aristotle was accused of impiety; but unlike Socrates he chose discretion rather than valour and absconded to his father's estate where he died the following year of a stomach complaint.

If Plato always writes out of a vision of a mystical and transcendent reality, Aristotle's message seems to be that what we see around us may well be all there is, so we should get to know it better. The ways in which he set about getting to know the natural world we have dealt with in chapter 2; here we can look at the way he tackled the philosophical problems that had occupied Plato and Socrates.

Central to Aristotle's thinking was his thought about the power of thought. Since it was the exercise of this power which set us above the animals, it had, in itself, a relationship with man's highest good, of which more later. But first, it was important to learn how to use this power correctly. He wrote a series of texts which are called his *Organon* (tool) which have the aim of teaching how to use the rational powers without making mistakes. Such books still seem to sell well and Aristotle covers the ground rather more extensively than the slim self-improvement paperbacks we can pick up today on our station bookstalls. In fact, it has to be admitted, the *Organon* is a tough read but here's something of the flavour of it: in *Categories* he distinguishes between a 'primary substance' and a 'secondary substance'. So, a 'primary substance' is a particular man, or horse, or tree, whereas the 'secondary substance' is the genus to which these primaries belong as 'horse', 'man' or 'tree'. Secondary substances do not have a concrete existence, and this is where Plato went wrong in attributing substantiality to qualities such as beauty, wisdom, etc.

In *Sophistical Refutations*, Aristotle has a go at sloppy thinking and sets out a series of forms of reasoning which are common but fallacious. Familiar to us is the circular argument: 'the soul lives on after death because it is immortal' and less familiar but still occasionally heard is the fallacy of the consequent: Drunkenness leads to destitution – Harry is destitute – therefore Harry is a drunk. To be aware of these pitfalls sharpens the powers of reasoning. They can be further organized by considering propositions in syllogistic form, and this Aristotle was particularly keen on. In fact he was the first philosopher to base an entire science of reasoning on the syllogism. The most famous of these is:

All men are mortal (major premiss)
Socrates is a man (minor premiss)
Therefore Socrates is mortal (conclusion)

The Latin mnemonic for this form of syllogism is 'Barbara'. Another is:

No flowers can talk
All roses are flowers
Therefore no roses can talk

This is 'Celarent'. And then there is 'Darii':

All men are rational
Some animals are men
Therefore some animals are rational

And there is 'Ferio':

No sumo wrestler is thin
Some men are Sumo wrestlers
Therefore some men are not thin.

There were others and they seem rigorous enough as mental exercises though, perhaps, limited as ways of getting to the heart of what matters. They did, apparently, quite serious damage to the evolution of the processes of rational thinking because Aristotelians held that they were the only possible approach to the truth. And thinkers all over Europe for centuries believed them. Their idea was that, since all deductive inference can be expressed in syllogisms, and since a strict adherence to syllogistic rules will exclude error, it should be possible to prove all that can be proved by simply following the rules. The most famous example of pushing Aristotelian logic into realms where it has no business to be is in the *Summa* of St Thomas Aquinas where a formidable intellect harnessed to the doctrine of reasoning developed by Aristotle finds itself involved in establishing the nature and composition of the bodies of angels and whether or not they can be in several places at the same time [*Summa Theologica* Part 1 Qs 50–53] and condemning incest between brother and sister on the ground that the affection of siblings added to that of husband and wife leads to over-frequent intercourse [*Summa Contra Gentiles* Book 3 Cap 124].

Having fine-tuned the intellectual faculties to seek truth and avoid error, how does Aristotle set about the serious business of ethics? He gave his mind to the problem and wrote treatises on it. Two have survived, the *Nicomachean Ethics* and the *Eudemian Ethics*, being collections of his lecture notes said to have been made by his son and his nephew respectively. They have been highly thought of: the French scholar

Brochard said that the 'Nicomachean Ethics was to eternal morality what Euclid's Elements was to geometry' [quoted Lévêque 1968; p 364].

And yet they seem to be, for the most part, commonplace, common-sense stuff. Aristotle has no time for moral absolutes and so his ethics are the study of what contributes to a man's good. The supreme good, according to Aristotle, is the attainment of happiness and he points out, as philosophers will, that this does not consist, as the common people think, in the possession of wealth or the experience of pleasure. It lies, he claims, in 'activity of the soul consonant with virtue'. So a good man is one whose activities are virtuous, which doesn't seem to take us very far.

He does try to help by pointing out that the highest virtue, in man, must be the exercise of that faculty which distinguishes him from the animals, namely the reason. And, since philosophers are most practised in the exercise of the reason, they are likely to be the most virtuous and therefore the happiest members of society. (Like so much of Aristotle this truth is arrived at by deduction and so was accepted, however much observation around the Lyceum, for example, might have given it the lie.)

If the highest happiness logically came from intellectual contemplation, then it was, of course, denied to the majority of men who are not capable of it; they have to be content with following one of the lesser virtues. And how could it be recognized? Aristotle wrote that it 'consists of a mean, peculiar to each person, defined by reason and such as a man of good sense would determine.' This seems to me to be another circular argument: we recognize a virtue because it is chosen by a man of good sense and we recognize his good sense because he has chosen a virtue. Aristotle again tries to help by defining moral virtues and claims they are always the mean between opposing vices, which are the excess and deficiency of the same quality. Now, this is quite neat if we consider that modesty comes somewhere between self-deprecation and boasting, or bravery between fool-hardiness and cowardice, or liberality between prodigality and mean-ness. But it surely doesn't apply to all the virtues. What about honesty, or truthfulness, or justice? Between which opposing excesses and deficiencies do they lie? To carry Aristotelian principles too far can lead to the error of the Mayor who, at his retirement party, announced with some pride in his farewell speech that he had always endeavoured to steer the narrow line between partiality on the one hand and impartiality on the other [quoted Russell 1945; p 173].

The Golden Mean has always been popular with middle-aged schoolmasters and others who are suspicious of enthusiasm and want us all to live balanced and rational lives, shunning excess. It's a principle that has to be carefully handled if life isn't to be deprived of spontaneity and one that we can all safely postpone until we get a little older.

Plato and Aristotle are the greatest of the philosophers who came after Socrates, but there were other disciples whose lives were changed by him and who went on to keep alive what they saw as of value in his teaching. Socrates founded no school of philosophy. Since he claimed to know nothing, this would have been out of character. But after his death his pupils set up on their own and started different, sometimes violently opposed schools which claimed to be based on his teaching. We shall look at two of them who have something to say to us today.

Cynics

Socrates had no more faithful pupil than Antisthenes, who, being born in Athens in 446, was about twenty-five years younger. Antisthenes had been a pupil of Gorgias, the rhetorician, and did not discover Socrates until he was a grown man. But then he made daily visits to hear Socrates, even though he lived in Piraeus and the round trip was a 16-kilometre (10-mile) walk. After Socrates was executed the rest of the pupils fled but Antisthenes remained, altered his lifestyle to fit in with his master's philosophy and taught his version of it at a school near Athens. His mother had been a slave from Thrace and so he taught in the *Kynosarges* school, which was for those whose blood was not pure Athenian.

Although Antisthenes wrote a lot, very little has survived and we have to rely on others, notably the historian of these philosophers, Diogenes Laertius, to reconstruct what he had to say.

He seems to have been initially attracted to Socrates, as were so many of his followers, by that preoccupation with getting to the heart of things that made him indifferent to inessentials. Socrates cared nothing for money, luxuries, even clothes, and Antisthenes was careful to sport a dirty and torn cloak as a sign of his discipleship. But, whereas Socrates thought little of material possessions because he was busy thinking about other things, Antisthenes erected the scorn for wealth into an ethical essential. This extension of the Socratic position came about because Antisthenes disagreed with his master over the question of virtue and knowledge. Socrates, you remember, made no distinction between them because he believed that no man would do wrong if he had the knowledge to choose the right. So virtue and knowledge were the same. Antisthenes saw that knowledge was only one of the influences on choice and that the others, appetites and desires, were frequently stronger and forced a man to choose the wrong. So he taught that the way to virtue was through the control of the appetites and the reduction of the desires.

It's a familiar problem to all of us. When we realize that we don't have enough income to buy all the things we want there are two alternatives: to increase our income or reduce our needs. Antisthenes would have pointed out that reducing our needs takes less effort. It is also more likely to be successful, since increased income brings with it increased needs and no matter how rich people get they still feel they need more:

As I see it, wealth is not a material possession that one can keep in one's house as if it were an object, but a disposition of the Soul; otherwise it would be impossible to explain why anyone who already possesses material goods should expose himself to peril and fatigue for no other reason than to acquire more wealth... For my part, though I confess I have no money at home, I don't want any because I only eat as much as will satisfy my hunger and drink to quench my thirst. I dress in such a way as to be as warm when out of doors as Callias with all his finery.   [XENOPHON, Symposium iv 34ff]

It was, of course, easier to simplify one's needs in fifth-century Athens.

We live in a society which spends a lot of money, skill and effort on persuading us that we can't live without a multitude of expensive inessentials and Antisthenes would have his work cut out to win a following anywhere in the western civilized world today. But perhaps, assailed as we are by commercials, we stand in particular need of his message.

Civilization, Antisthenes taught, was the enemy of the ideally simple life. The man who had found virtue through frugality and self-denial could only be turned aside from the true path by the distractions of civilized life. So he was the model for Rousseau and for all the bucolic crusaders who have preached a return to rural simplicity.

The most famous of his followers was Diogenes of Sinope who lived a simpler life than any other man, philosopher or not. He saw that Antisthenes had not lived up to his own theories and called him 'a trumpet that hears nothing but itself'. If you really are indifferent to the comforts of civilized life, then the least you can do is live without them. This he did. In fact, Diogenes is remembered more for his way of life than for his philosophy. He is famous for living in a tub and for touring the streets of Athens carrying a lighted lantern in broad daylight proclaiming that he was on the look out for an honest man. The tub for which he became famous may well have been a large pitcher, of the sort used, in primitive times, to bury people in, which would have made his home a sort of *memento mori*, rather like sleeping in a coffin. That would certainly have fitted his character well. Diogenes taught that the individual must be self-sufficient and not rely on society in any way. When he saw a boy drinking water out of his hands he threw away his drinking cup. When Alexander the Great came across him sunbathing one day and asked if he, the most powerful ruler in the world, could be of any service to the destitute philosopher, Diogenes replied simply: 'Yes. Get out of my sunlight.'

To a Socratic scorn for possessions, Diogenes added a contempt for the politenesses of civilized society, which he saw as simple insincerities. He thought that Prometheus had been quite rightly punished because he brought to Mankind the arts which have resulted in so much pretension and artificiality. He was the prototypic plain blunt man, quick to spot pretension and pious hypocrisy. Although he dressed in rags and laughed at the wealthy for their concern with fine clothes, he turned on a group of Spartans who paraded in the city wearing dirty clothes as a public protest against the extravagances of wealth: 'There goes another kind of pride,' he said [quoted Hooper 1968; p 441].

While Plato and Aristotle sought to refine life and to seek for truth and order in the intellectual disciplines of the Academy and the Lyceum, Diogenes believed that a man could only find peace through a retreat from civilization into self-examination and self-reliance. All the grand schemes for the organization of society were doomed by the selfishness and hypocrisy of men.

Because Diogenes and his followers lived in extreme poverty and, in defiance of the manners of polite society, scratched themselves wherever they itched whenever they felt like it, they were called Cynics from the Greek word 'kynikos' which means 'like a dog'. Diogenes called himself the 'Dog' and held up the life of animals as the true model which mankind should follow. (There is a duller explanation: that the name came from the school of Kynosarges, where Antisthenes taught.) There's an irony in the fact that the name given to these philosophers who despised material possessions was used by Wilde's Lord Darlington of 'a man who knows the price of everything and the value of nothing'.

The spirit of Diogenes, misanthropic and embittered as he seems to be, lived on in those who sought sanctity through poverty inside and outside the world's great religions. It may seem unlikely that the ideals which drove a man to live in a barrel two and a half thousand years ago have much relevance to us today, but Diogenes valued and was searching for the true worth of human beings when stripped of their social disguises. And there is a lasting relevance in his claim 'It is a mark of God to need nothing, and of those who are like God to need little.'

Cyrenaics

If Diogenes and the Cynics behaved like dogs, the Cyrenaics modelled themselves on cats. The famous confrontation between leaders of the two schools illustrates this well. Diogenes was washing turnip tops at a well when Aristippus of Cyrene passed by. 'If you learned to eat greens,' shouted Diogenes, 'you wouldn't have to flatter the tyrants.' 'And if you knew how to flatter the tyrants,' replied Aristippus, 'you wouldn't have to eat greens.'

Aristippus attacked the notion that there is virtue in deprivation. In fact, he taught that pleasure was a good thing and should be sought. We ought to satisfy our appetites so long as they do not gain control over us. So he justifies his visits to a prostitute by saying 'I possess her but am not possessed by her', and said that there was nothing shameful about visiting a brothel – only about not being able to leave it. There is another story contrasting his attitude with that of Diogenes in which the Cyrenaic comes out best: on leaving the public baths, he put on Diogenes' dirty and torn cloak as a joke and left behind his own. Diogenes preferred to walk back to his barrel naked rather than wear the rich purple of Aristippus.

So the contrast was between the Cynic, who refused contact with finery, as he did with all the unnecessary pleasures of life, and the Cyrenaic who believed in enjoying what he could get, without becoming dependent on his pleasures. It seems to me that the Cyrenaics would have been the school to join, but later members went off the rails: Theodorus the Atheist taught that individual acts of self-gratification are morally indifferent and that no sensible man would die for his country. Theft, adultery and whatever takes your fancy are fine so long as 'circumstances permit'. Hegesias seems to have had no fun at all from teaching a doctrine of self-gratification. He thought life was so miserable that the best we could do is to avoid discomfort and the surest way of doing that is to commit suicide. He was known as *peisithanatos*, the man who persuades to the death. He must have been quite successful: few of his followers survived.

Philosophical Chart

Sophists

PROTAGORAS of Abdera	**490–420**
('Man is the measure of all things')	
GORGIAS of Leontini	*c.* **485–***c.* **380**
('On the Non-existent')	
PRODICOS of Ceos	**470–?**
ANTIPHON of Athens	**5th cent.**
CRITIAS of Athens	**460–403**
(political theorist)	

Socrates and popular philosophy

SOCRATES	**470–399**
('I know one thing: that I know nothing')	
XENOPHON of Athens	**428–354**
AESCHINES	**5th–4th cent.**
SIMMIAS of Thebes	**5th–4th cent.**

Plato and the academy

PLATO	**429–347**
SPEUSIPPOS	**407–339**
EUDOXOS of Cnidos	**390–340**
XENOCRATES of Chalcedon	**395–315**

Aristotle and the peripatetics

ARISTOTLE	**384–322**
THEOPHRASTOS of Lesbos	**372–288**
ARISTOXENOS of Taras	**375–?**

Cynics

ANTISTHENES of Athens	**445–360**
DIOGENES of Sinope	**412–323**

Cyrenaics

ARISTIPPUS of Cyrene	**435–355**
ARETE (his daughter)	**4th cent.**
ARISTIPPUS the Younger (son of Arete)	**4th cent.**
THEODORUS the atheist	**4th–3rd cent.**
HEGESIAS the *peisithanatos*	**4th–3rd cent.**

Epilogue

One of the consequences of living in the Age of Hype is that we don't know what to take seriously any more. Banner headlines in our daily papers announce the minor sexual indiscretion of a middle-ranking politician; fanfares herald a new breakfast cereal; blazing lights and thunderous applause usher on to our television screens, not the Sultan of Brunei or the Emperor of Japan but the genial host of our weekly games show. When so much ado is made about nothing, there's little left with which to make ado about something.

It is just possible, by a constant and unwavering inattention, to escape the worst effects of this incessant battering, this constant urging to take seriously the commonplace, to be awed by the trivial; but most of us don't have the energy to look away all the time and we end up confused, demoralized and desensitized. A palliative for this condition is to spend a few hours at the end of each day in a darkened and soundproof room soaking in bath water at blood temperature; a cure is to go back to the Greeks. The one thing you can be absolutely sure of when coming up against classical Greek culture today is that the content is going to be worth more than the packaging. A slim paperback will contain some of the most subtle and profound thoughts that have yet arisen in the human reason and imagination, promptings from an age when all voices had the same carrying power, when the substance of the message and not the loudness with which it was proclaimed won attention. These voices carry us back from the glitzy fringes to the essential heart of things.

A Few Good Books

Recommending books is a dangerous business, like recommending friends. It's the same thing, really, because if we don't have to read a particular book for an exam or as part of a study course, we stay with it only if we get along with the author. And this is a very personal thing: what to one person is lively and entertaining might be to another unbearably flippant, and an approach which to one shows a proper seriousness of purpose, to another seems stunningly dull.

But it always strikes me as unhelpful when we get to the end of a book and are faced by an impersonal list of titles and authors with no hint as to their readability. There are good books which can be enjoyed on the beach or the back of a bus; there are others which shouldn't be tackled without a good night's sleep followed by a really sustaining breakfast. And there are, I suspect, seminal works of such bulk and density that, although they turn up in every bibliography, nobody has quite managed to get through them.

These are the books I enjoyed most. The ones in the bibliography you can borrow from a good library; these are worth spending money on:

Chapter 1 As a general introduction to the historical background, I like very much the *Oxford History of the Classical World* which is a satisfyingly fat, well illustrated book of essays that demand no previous knowledge. It ranges far beyond history. My favourite of the shorter works is H. D. F. Kitto's little Penguin of 1951, *The Greeks*, which has wit and insight wrapped up in old-fashioned charm. To take the subject more earnestly, it's worth tackling another book of the same name by Antony Andrewes published by Hutchinson sixteen years later. As a general handbook, covering the whole background to classical Athenian culture, it's hard to beat *The World of Athens*, by the Joint Association of Classical Teachers (JACT). Anyone who, like myself, was brought up to believe the classical Greeks were like those who teach about them, will profit immensely from E.R. Dodds, *The Greeks and the Irrational*.

As for Homer, there are plenty of background introductions: the more lively and comprehensible I found to be Chapter 3 of Albin Lesky's *History of Greek Literature* and Chapter 1 of Peter Levi's *Pelican History of Greek Literature*. It's advisable to avoid the theorizing about authorship and even the literary criticism and get straight down to the text, which brings us to the question of translations. Here the style is such a personal matter that it's difficult to recommend. But the choice is between the grand style of the American poets Richmond Lattimore (Chicago 1951, 1965) and Robert Fitzgerald (Oxford 1984) or the high prose of Walter Shewring (Oxford 1980), and the more accessible prose of E.V. Rieu in Penguin Classics which has been accused of turning Homer into Trollope. The *Odyssey* has been revised by his son, with Peter Jones, and is a spanking good read. There is a more recent Penguin Classic by Martin Hammond which is lively. Herodotus and Thucydides are both available in Penguin translations with good introductions.

Chapter 2 A readable survey of Greek science is in the early chapters of the *Cambridge Illustrated History of the World's Science*, edited by Colin Ronan. There is more detail in the books of Charles Singer, *Greek Biology and Greek Medicine* (1922), and the relevant chapters of *Studies in the History and Method of Science* (1921). The books of G.E.R. Lloyd, *Early Greek Science* and *Magic, Reason and Experience* go into more detail but always in a lively and interesting way.

Chapter 3 F.A. Wright's little book *Greek Athletics* is, perhaps more enthusiastic than scholarly but covers the ground. More full in its detail is H.A. Harris, *Greek Athletes and Athletics*, and there is an excellent survey in M. I. Finley and H. W. Pleket's *The Olympic Games* (1976) but I had to rely on sources in modern Greek for much of the information here. When it comes to sculpture, there is a wide choice stretching back in time; the secret is to avoid the writers who go on about planes and angles or the ones obsessed by attributions. I very much enjoy Kenneth Clark's *The Nude*, which is driven by a great enthusiasm for the subject. Gisela Richter's *Sculpture and Sculptors of the Greeks* is a good general survey but, if you can't get to the galleries and have to rely on photographs, it's worth getting John Boardman's *Greek Sculpture: archaic period* and *Greek Sculpture: classical period* for the sake of the illustrations.

There is a steady output of animated stuff on sex: David Halperin's *One Hundred Years of Homosexuality*, and John Winkler's *The Constraints of Desire* are unapologetically campaigning works and I was grateful for the dispassionate approach – not the easiest in this subject – of Sir Kenneth Dover's *Greek Homosexuality*.

The position of women is discussed in W. K. Lacey, *The Family in Classical Greece* and Sarah Pomeroy's splendidly titled *Goddesses, Whores, Wives and Slaves*. There is a survey of the problems in Roger Just, *Women in Athenian Law and Life*. Both these latter have good bibliographies.

Chapter 4 The politics of Greece must have threatened many a rain forest. I find the subject is best approached through a general-purpose survey such as the *Oxford History of the Classical World* or the schematic *The World of Athens* put out by JACT. Although admitting to a low threshold of boredom in this subject area, I was held by Victor Ehrenberg's *The Greek State*, which I picked up because I saw it described as 'essential reading', and H. D. F. Kitto managed, by stylistic graces and a sprinkling of wit, to keep my attention to the end of *The Greeks*. Those with more stamina might enjoy W. G. Forrest, *The Emergence of Greek Democracy* or even J. K. Davies, *Democracy and Classical Greece*, but they should be warned that the battle over what and whether Athenian democracy was, rages on in the pages of learned journals.

There are surveys of the Greek dramatists in Albin Lesky, *History of Greek Literature* and Peter Levi, *The Pelican History of Greek Literature*. But it is essential to read the plays first, before trying to set them in any sort of literary or historical context. Either they will work for you on the printed page or they won't. If they don't, it's just hard work trying to bone up on their significance in the development of literature or the history of the theatre. If they do, everything about them then becomes interesting. As for translations, the best ones to start on are the most modern in the Penguin Classics because they set up fewest barriers for today's readers. Once you're hooked you can enjoy the richness of W. B. Yeats and Ezra Pound. You might then enjoy Richmond Lattimore's insights in *The Poetry of Greek Tragedy* and those of an expert in modern drama in Brian Vickers, *Towards Greek Tragedy: drama, myth, society.*

Chapter 5 There's a plethora [Greek *plithore*: medical term meaning 'any unhealthy repletion or excess' O.E.D.] of books on Greek philosophy. All of the standard Histories have opening chapters giving surveys in greater or lesser detail. The most readable is Bertrand Russell, *History of Western Philosophy*, although it helps to remember that the author was dismissed for superficiality after delivering the lectures on which it is based. I always enjoy Frederick Copleston's *A History of Philosophy*, as a way of clearing the head after reading Bertrand Russell. Luciano de Crescenzo, *The History of Greek Philosophy*, is a very funny book with delightful anecdotes but the author doesn't always resist the temptation to make his quotations fit the point they're meant to illustrate. As to more specialist works, the early philosophers have been well covered in Kirk and Raven, *The Presocratic Philosophers* which has plenty of texts all translated and also E. Hussey, *The Presocratics*, which assumes no knowledge of Greek.

The secondary literature on Plato and Aristotle is, of course, prodigious and best left alone until you've read the major texts which are easily available in translations in the Penguin Classics series and have excellent introductions.

Bibliography of references

Aeschylus,   The Oresteian Trilogy, trans. by Philip Vellacott, Penguin, 1956; reissued 1959

Andrewes, Antony,   The Greeks, Hutchinson, 1967

Aristophanes,   The Assembly Women, trans. by David Barrett, in Birds and other plays, Penguin, 1988

Aristophanes,   Lysistrata and other plays, trans. by Alan H. Sommerstein, Penguin, 1973

Aristotle,   Ethics, trans. by J. A. K. Thomson, revised by Hugh Tredennick, with introduction and bibliography by Jonathan Barnes, Penguin, 1976

Aristotle,   Parts of Animals, trans. by A. L. Peck; with Movement of Animals and Progression of Animals, trans. by E. S. Forster, (Loeb Classical Library) Harvard University Press, 1945

Aristotle,   Generation of Animals, trans. by A. L. Peck, (Loeb Classical Library) Heinemann, 1943

Aristotle,   History of Animals, trans. by D. M. Balme (Loeb Classical Library), Harvard University Press, 1991

Arnott, Peter D.   An Introduction to the Greek World, Macmillan, 1967

Auden, W. H.,   'The Greeks and us' in Forewords and afterwords, Faber, 1973; pbk., 1979

Boardman, John,   Greek Sculpture: archaic period, Thames & Hudson, 1978

Boardman, John,   Greek Sculpture: classical period, Thames & Hudson, 1985. op; pbk., 1987

Boardman, John, Griffin, Jasper and Murray, Oswyn (eds.),	*The Oxford History of the Classical World*, Oxford University Press, 1986; in 2 vols, pbk., 1988
Bowder, Diana R.,	*Who Was Who in the Greek World*, Phaidon, 1980
Bowra, C. M.,	*The Greek Experience*, Weidenfeld & Nicolson, 1957; pbk., 1985
Browning, Robert (ed.),	*The Greek World: Classical, Byzantine and Modern*, Thames & Hudson, 1985
Clagett, Marshall,	*Greek Science in Antiquity*, Abelard-Schuman, 1957; reissued 1976
Clark, Kenneth,	*The Nude*, John Murray, 1957
Constantine, David J.,	*Early Greek Travellers and the Hellenic Ideal*, Cambridge University Press, 1984
Copleston, Frederick,	*A History of Philosophy*, 9 vol. set, New York, Search Press, 1966; individual vols., New York, Search Press, 1952–75
Crawford, Michael H. & Whitehead, David,	*Archaic and Classical Greece: selection of ancient sources in translation*, Cambridge University Press, 1983
Crescenzo, Luciano de,	*History of Greek Philosophy*, (Picador) Pan, 1989; pbk., 1991
Davies, J. K.,	*Democracy and Classical Greece*, Hassocks, Harvester, 1978; Fontana, 1978
Detienne, M. & Vernant, J. P.,	*Cunning Intelligence in Greek Culture and Society*, Hassocks, Harvester, 1978; University of Chicago Press, 1991
Dickinson, G. Lowes,	*The Greek View of Life*, Methuen, 1896; Methuen, 23rd ed., 1957
Dickinson, G. Lowes,	*Plato and his Dialogues*, Allen & Unwin, 1931; (Pelican) Penguin, 1947
Dodds, E. R.,	*The Greeks and the Irrational*, University of California Press: Cambridge University Press, 1951; pbk., 1951
Dover, K. J.,	*Greek Homosexuality*, Duckworth, 1978; pbk., 1978
Dover, K. J.,	*The Greeks*, BBC, 1980; Oxford University Press, 1982
Ehrenberg, Victor,	*The Greek State*, Blackwell, 1960; Methuen, 2nd rev. ed., 1969
Euripides,	*Medea and other plays*, trans. by Philip Vellacott, Penguin, 1963

Farrington, Benjamin, *Greek Science,* (Pelican) Penguin, 1944; Spokesman, hbk. and pbk., 1981

Finley, M. I., *The Ancient Greeks,* Chatto & Windus, 1963; Penguin, 1991

Finley, M. I., *The Legacy of Greece: a new appraisal,* Oxford University Press, 1981; pbk., 1984

Flaceliere, Robert, *Daily Life in Greece at the Time of Pericles,* Weidenfeld & Nicolson, 1965

Forrest, W. G., *The Emergence of Greek Democracy,* Weidenfeld & Nicolson, 1966

Gombrich, Ernst, *The Story of Art,* Phaidon, 1991

Grant, Michael, *The Classical Greeks,* Weidenfeld & Nicolson, 1989

Halperin, David, *One Hundred Years of Homosexuality,* Routledge, hbk. and pbk., 1990

Harris, H. A., *Greek Athletes and Athletics,* Hutchinson, 1964

Herodotus, *The Histories,* trans. by Aubrey de Selincourt, revised by A. R. Burn, Penguin, 1972

Hippocrates, *The Genuine Works of Hippocrates,* trans. by Francis Adams, Bailliere, 1939

Homer, *The Iliad,* trans. by Martin Hammond, Penguin, 1987

Homer, *The Odyssey,* trans. by E. V. Rieu, revised by D. C. H. Rieu in consultation with Peter V. Jones, Penguin, 1991

Hooper, Finley, *Greek realities: life and thought in ancient Greece,* Hart-Davis, 1968

Hussey, E., *The presocratics* (Classical Life & Letters), Duckworth, 1972; pbk., 1974

JACT: Joint Association of Classical Teachers, *The World of Athens: An Introduction to Classical Athenian Culture,* Cambridge University Press, hbk. and pbk., 1984

Just, Roger, *Women in Athenian Law and Life,* Routledge, 1989; pbk., 1991

Kirk, G. S. & Raven, J. E., *The Presocratic Philosophers,* Cambridge University Press, 1957; 2nd rev. ed., 1983

Kitto, H. D. F., *The Greeks,* (Pelican) Penguin, 1951; Penguin, 1991

Istoria tou Ellenikou Ethnous, Athens, Ekdotike Athenon, 1971

Lacey, W. K., *The Family in Classical Greece,* Thames & Hudson, 1968

Lattimore, Richmond, The Poetry of Greek Tragedy, Baltimore, Johns Hopkins Press, 1958

Leckie, Ross, Bluff Your Way in the Classics, (Bluffer's Guide) Ravette, 1989

Lesky, Albin, History of Greek Literature, Methuen, 1966

Lévêque, Pierre, The Greek Adventure, Weidenfeld & Nicolson, 1968

Levi, Peter, Atlas of the Greek World, Phaidon, 1984

Levi, Peter, Pelican History of Greek Literature, (Pelican) Penguin, 1985

Livingstone, R. W., Greek Genius and its Meaning, Clarendon, 1912

Livingstone, R. W. (ed.), The Legacy of Greece, Clarendon, 1921; Oxford University Press, 1969

Lloyd, G. E. R., Early Greek Science: Thales to Aristotle, Chatto and Windus, 1970; W. W. Norton, 1974

Lloyd, G. E. R., Magic, Reason and Experience, Cambridge University Press, hbk. and pbk., 1979

Lloyd, G. E. R., Methods and Problems in Greek Science, Cambridge University Press, 1991

Lloyd-Jones, Hugh, Greek in a Cold Climate, Duckworth, 1991

Lloyd-Jones, Hugh, The Greeks, Watts, 1962

Lunn, Sir H. (ed.), Aegean Civilisations, Ernest Benn, 1925

Mahaffy, J. P., What have the Greeks done for Modern Civilisation? New York, Putnam, 1909

Medawar, P. B. & J. S., Aristotle to Zoos: a Philosophical Dictionary of Biology, Weidenfeld & Nicolson, 1984

Plato, The Last Days of Socrates, trans. by Hugh Tredennick, Penguin, 1969

Plato, The Laws, trans. by Trevor J. Saunders, Penguin, 1970; reprinted 1975

Pomeroy, S. B., Goddesses, Whores, Wives and Slaves, New York, Schoken, 1975; Hale, 1976

Richter, Gisela, Handbook of Greek Art, Phaidon, 1959; 9th rev. ed., 1989

Richter, Gisela, The Sculpture and Sculptors of the Greeks, Yale University Press, 4th rev. ed., 1970, op

Robertson, Martin, A Shorter History of Greek Art, Cambridge University Press, 1981; pbk., 1981

Ronan, Colin,   Cambridge Illustrated History of the World's Science, Cambridge
University Press, 1983

Russell, Bertrand,   History of Western Philosophy, Allen & Unwin, 1946; Routledge,
1991; new edn. of 2nd edn., Routledge, 1992

Sophocles,   Electra and other plays, trans. E. F. Watling, Penguin, 1953

Spencer, Terence,   Fair Greece, Sad Relic: literary Philhellenism from Shakespeare to Byron,
Weidenfeld & Nicolson, 1954

Stobart, J. C.,   The Glory that was Greece, Sidgwick & Jackson, 1911; 4th rev.
edn., 1964

Taplin, Oliver,   Greek Fire, Cape, 1989

Temple, William   Plato and Christianity, Macmillan, 1916

Thucydides,   History of the Peloponnesian War, trans. Rex Warner, Penguin,
1972

Tsigakou, F-M.,   The Rediscovery of Greece, Thames & Hudson, 1981

Tsougarakis, Helen   The Eve of the Greek Revival: British travellers' perceptions of early 19th
Angelomatis-,   century Greece, Routledge, 1990

Vickers, Brian,   Towards Greek Tragedy: drama, myth, society, (Vol. 1 of Comparative
Tragedy), Longman, 1973

Winkler, John J.,   The Constraints of Desire: anthropology of sex and gender in Ancient
Greece, Routledge 1990; pbk., 1990

Wright, F. A.,   Greek Athletics, Cape, 1925

Picture Credits

Index